Copyright © 2020 by Chikku Publishing

All rights reserved. No part of this book may be reproduced or used in any manner without written permission of the copyright owner except for the use of quotations in a book review. For more information, address: chikku@theckpublishing.com

FIRST EDITION

This Beach Coloring Book Belongs To

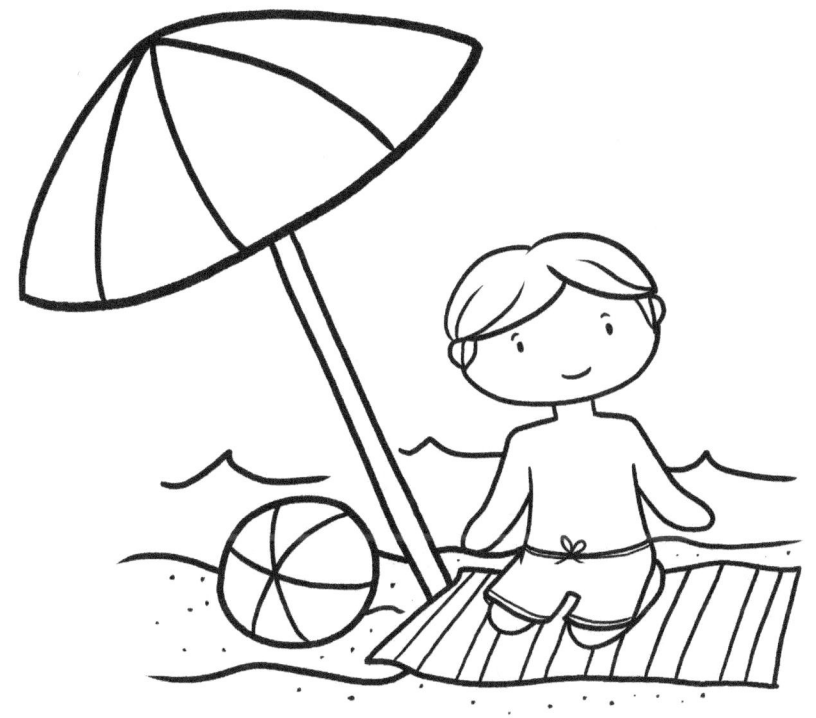

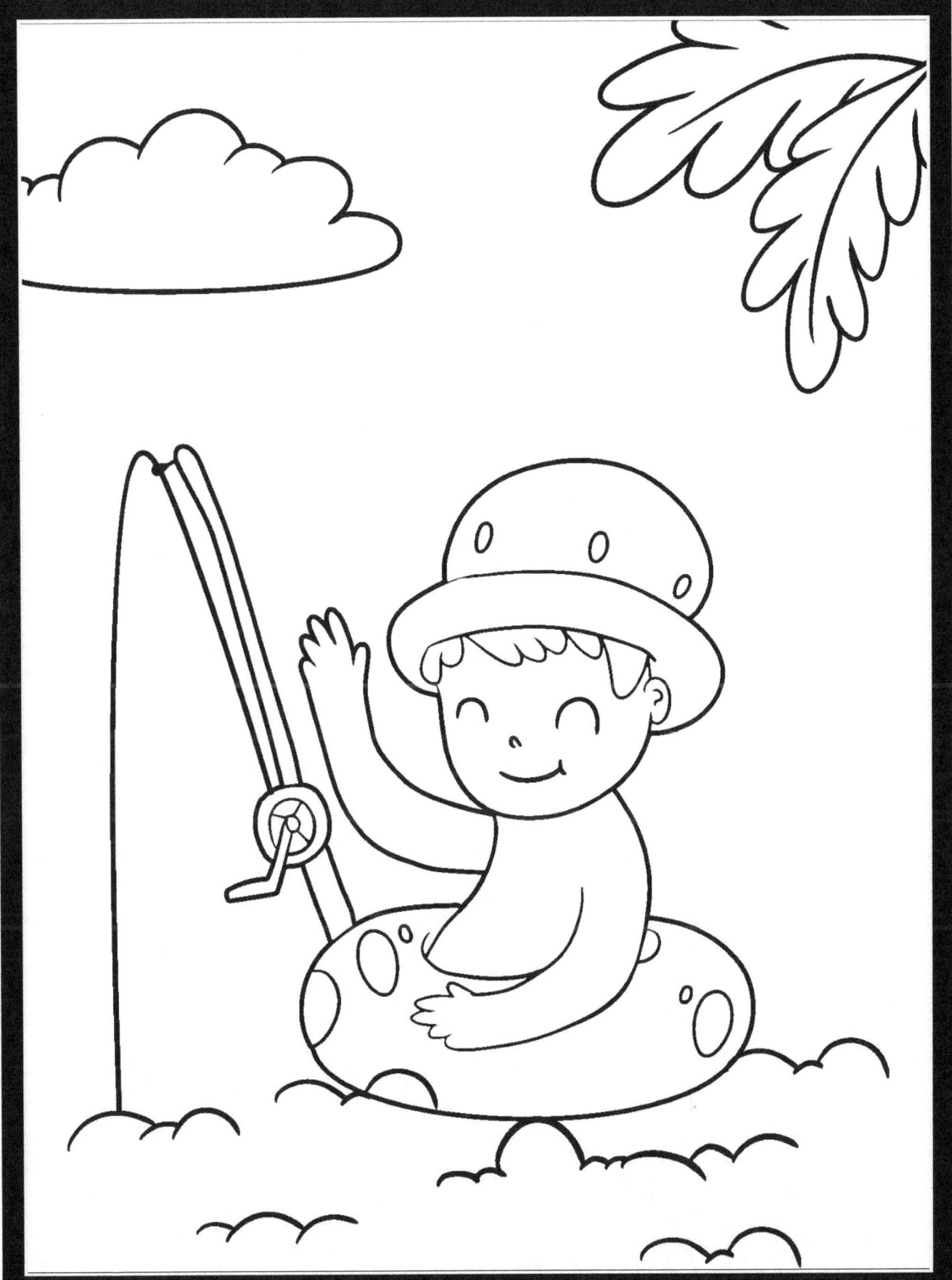

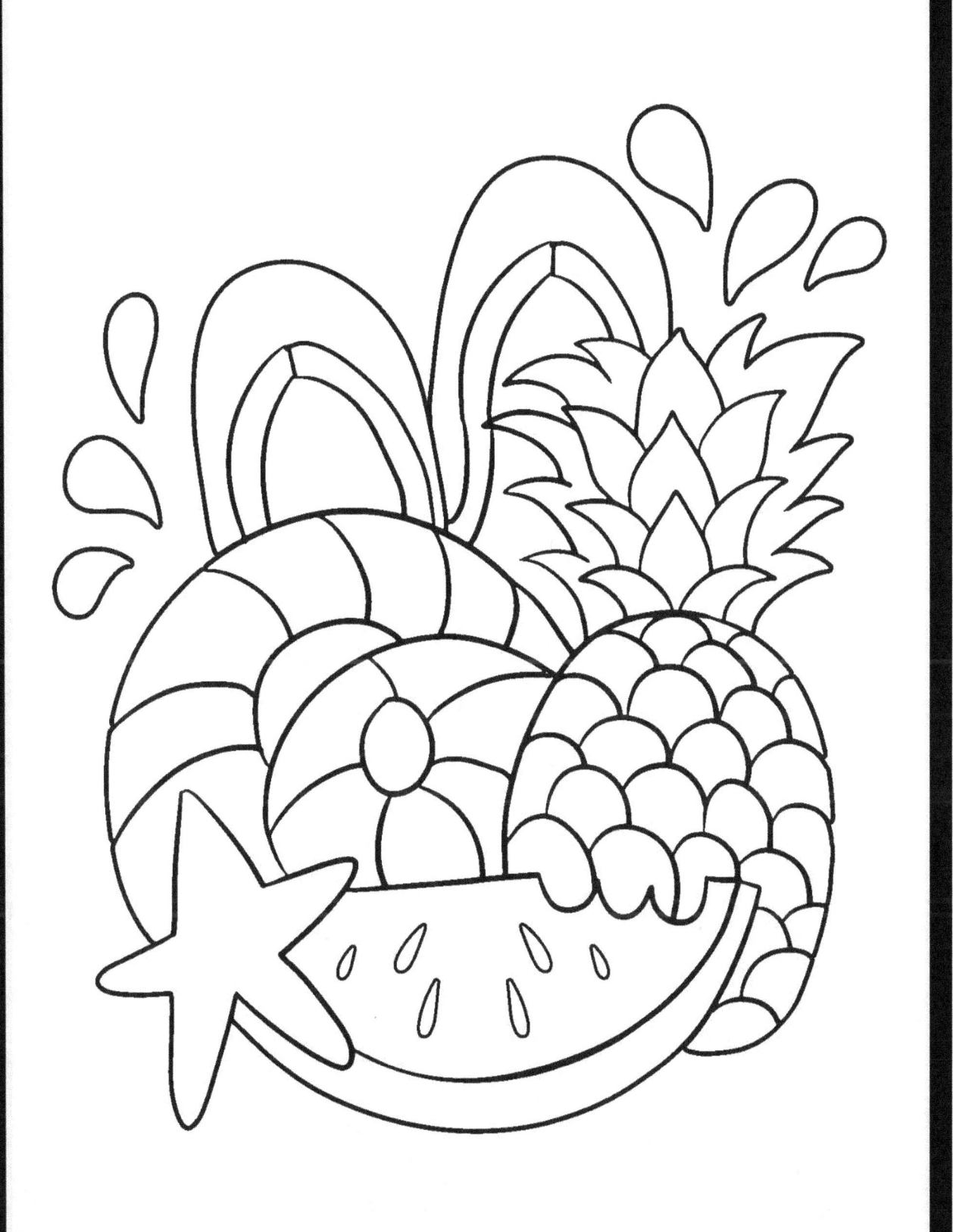

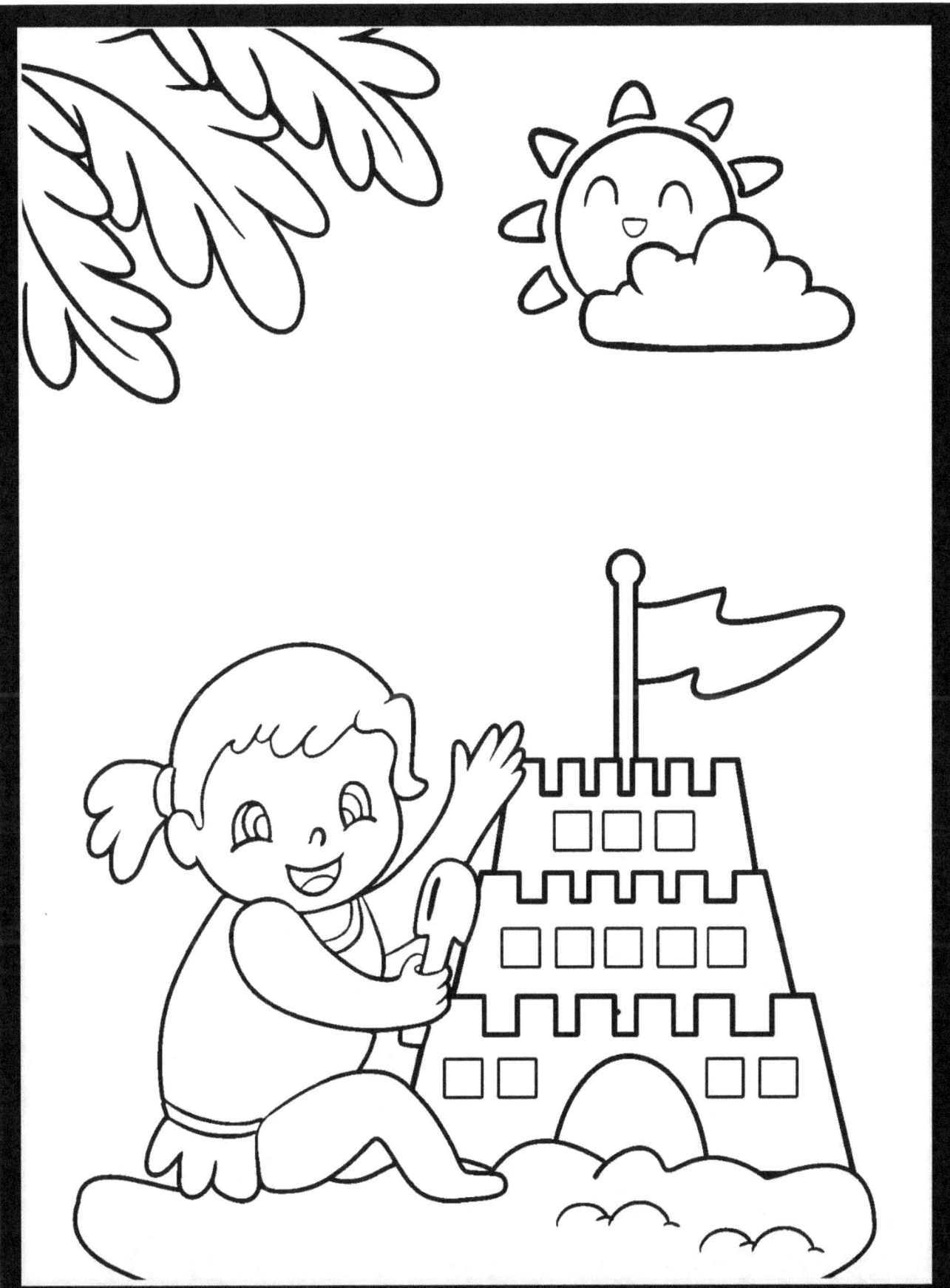

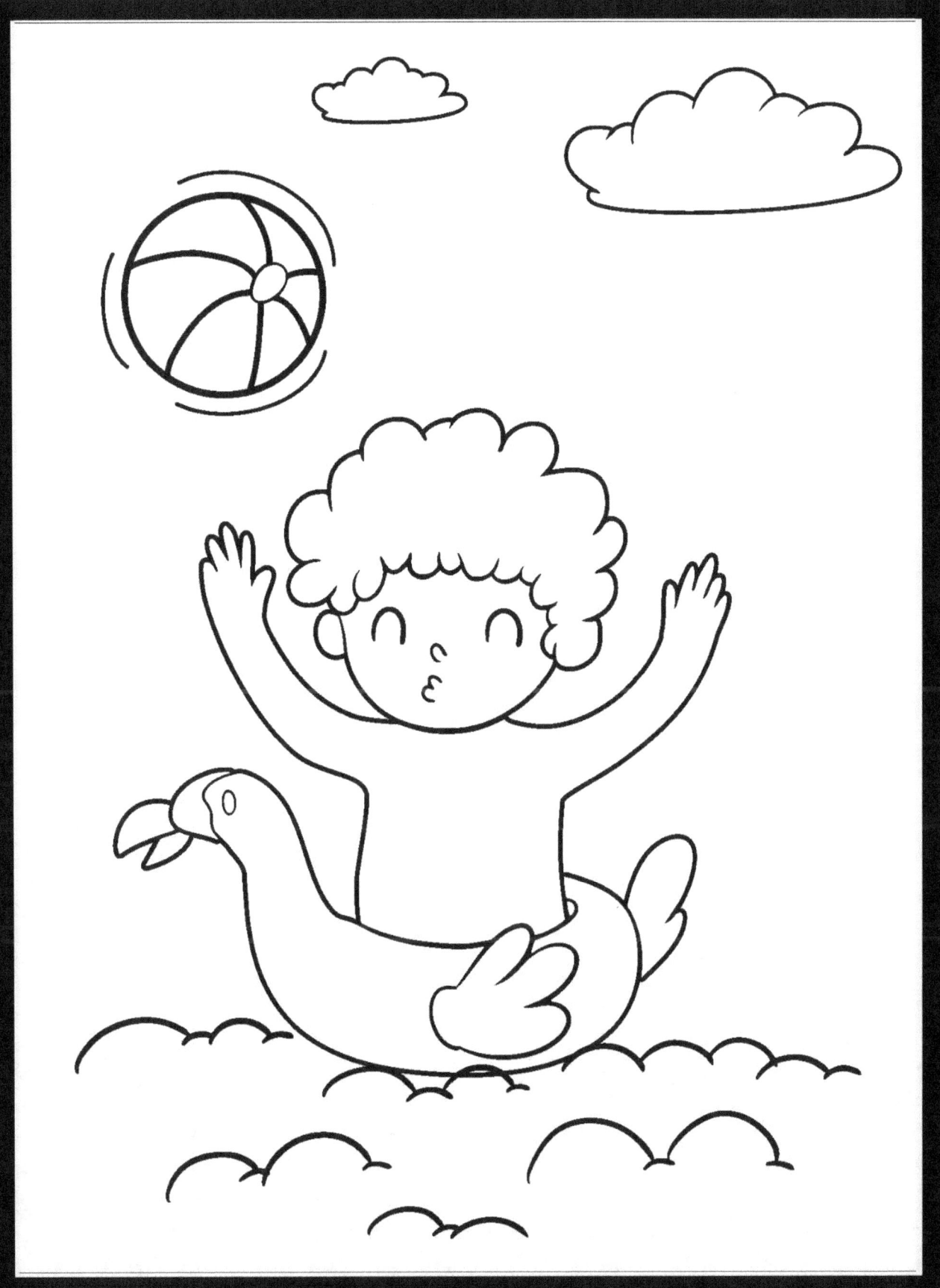

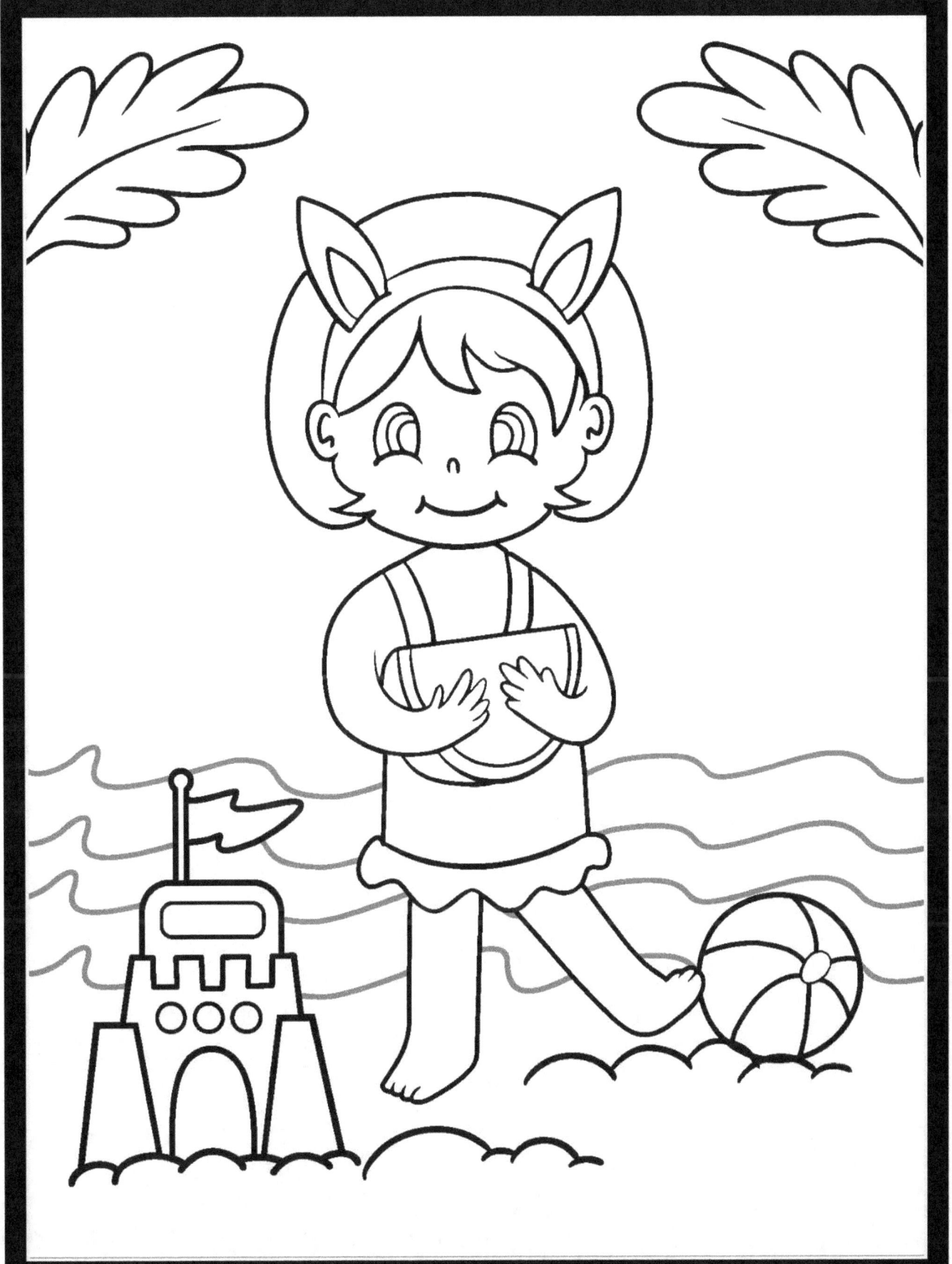

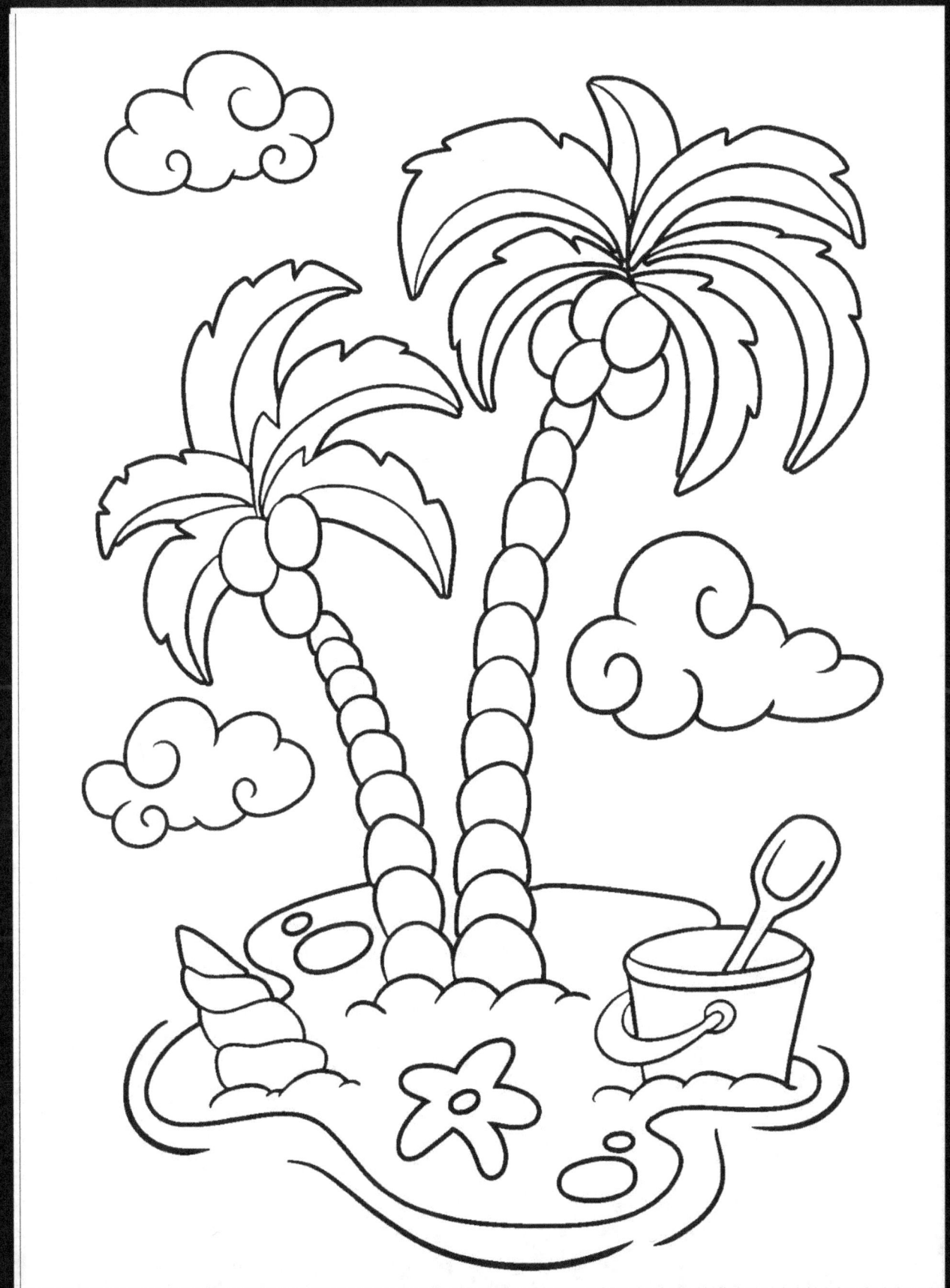

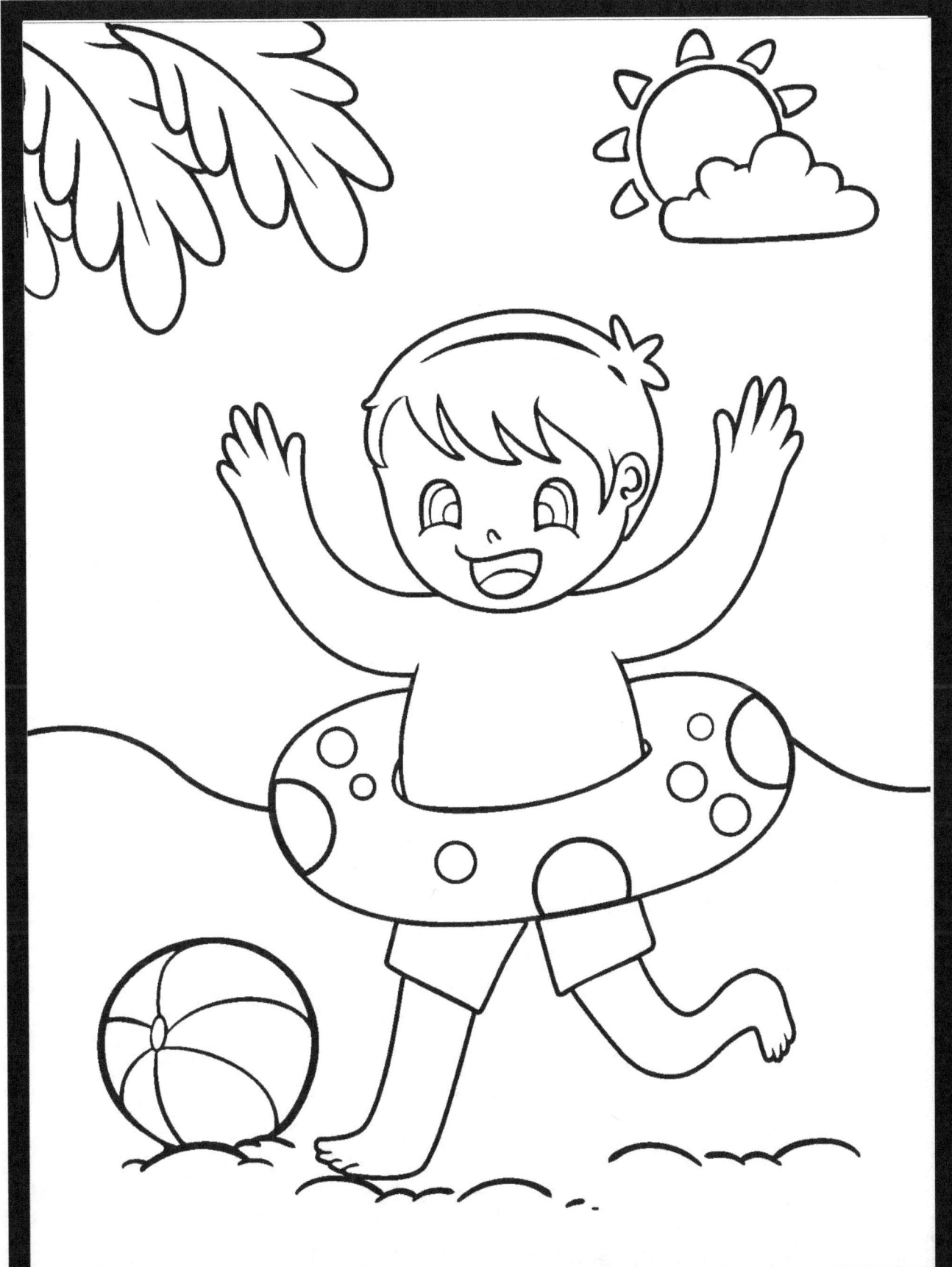

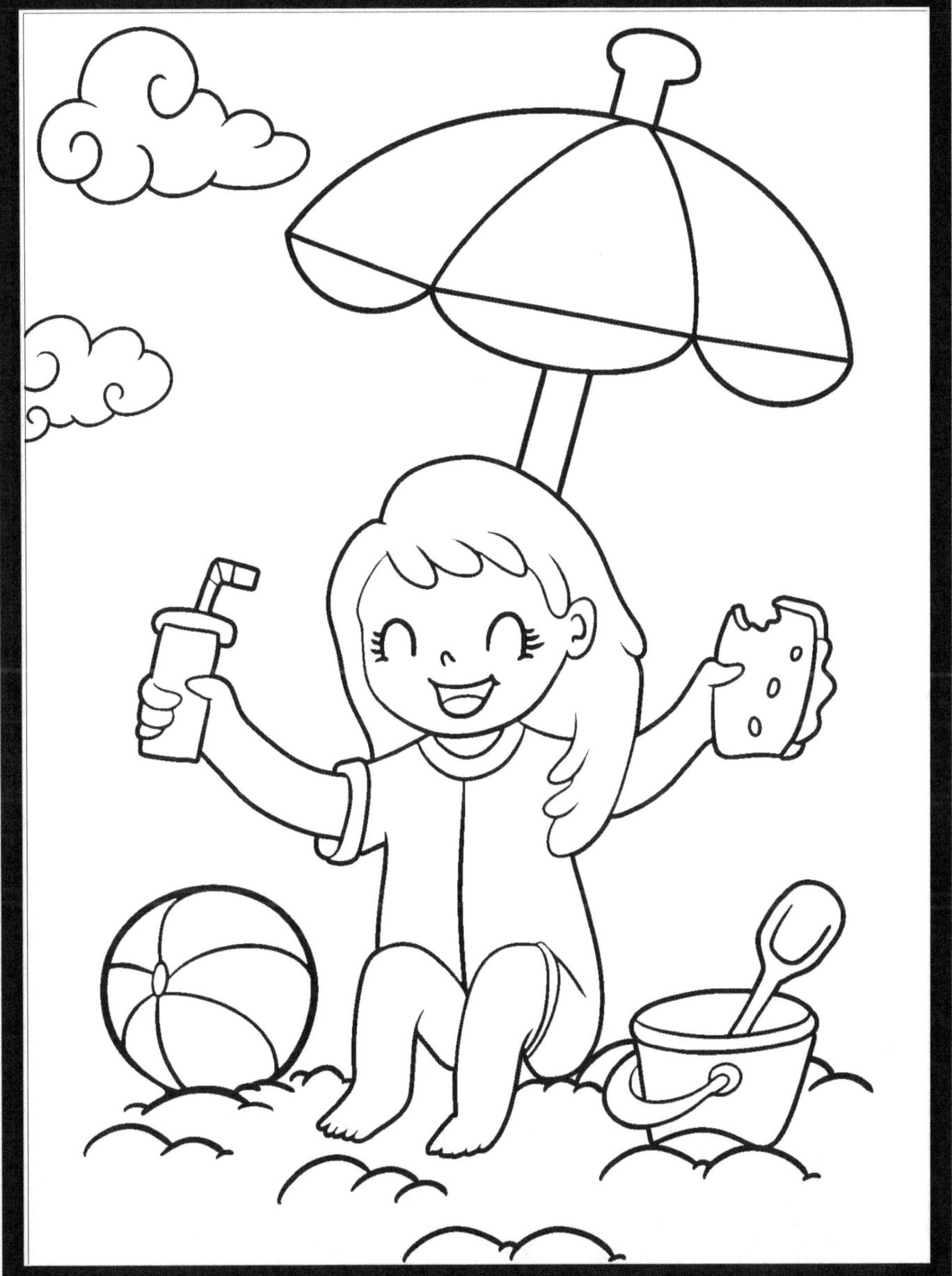

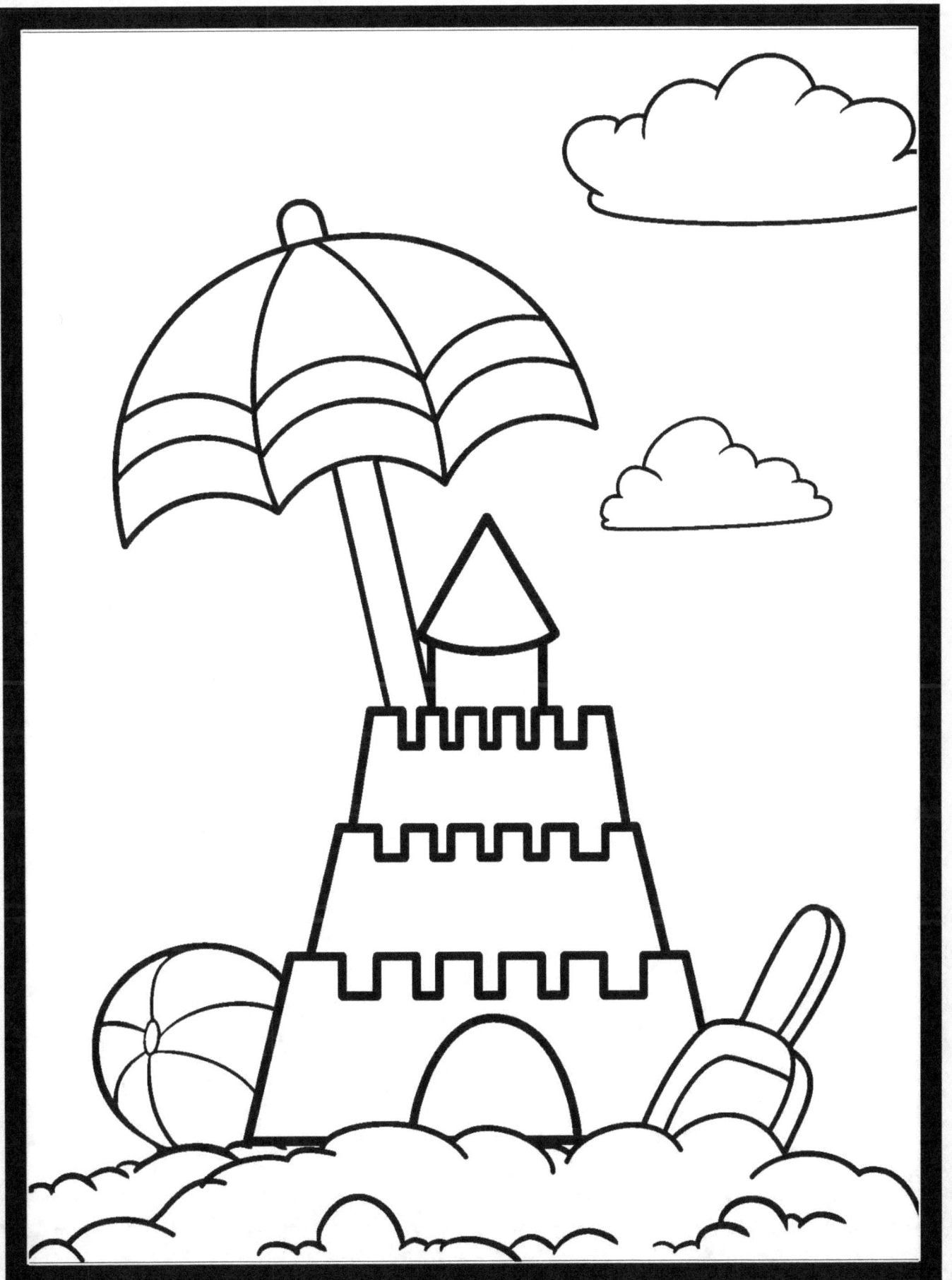

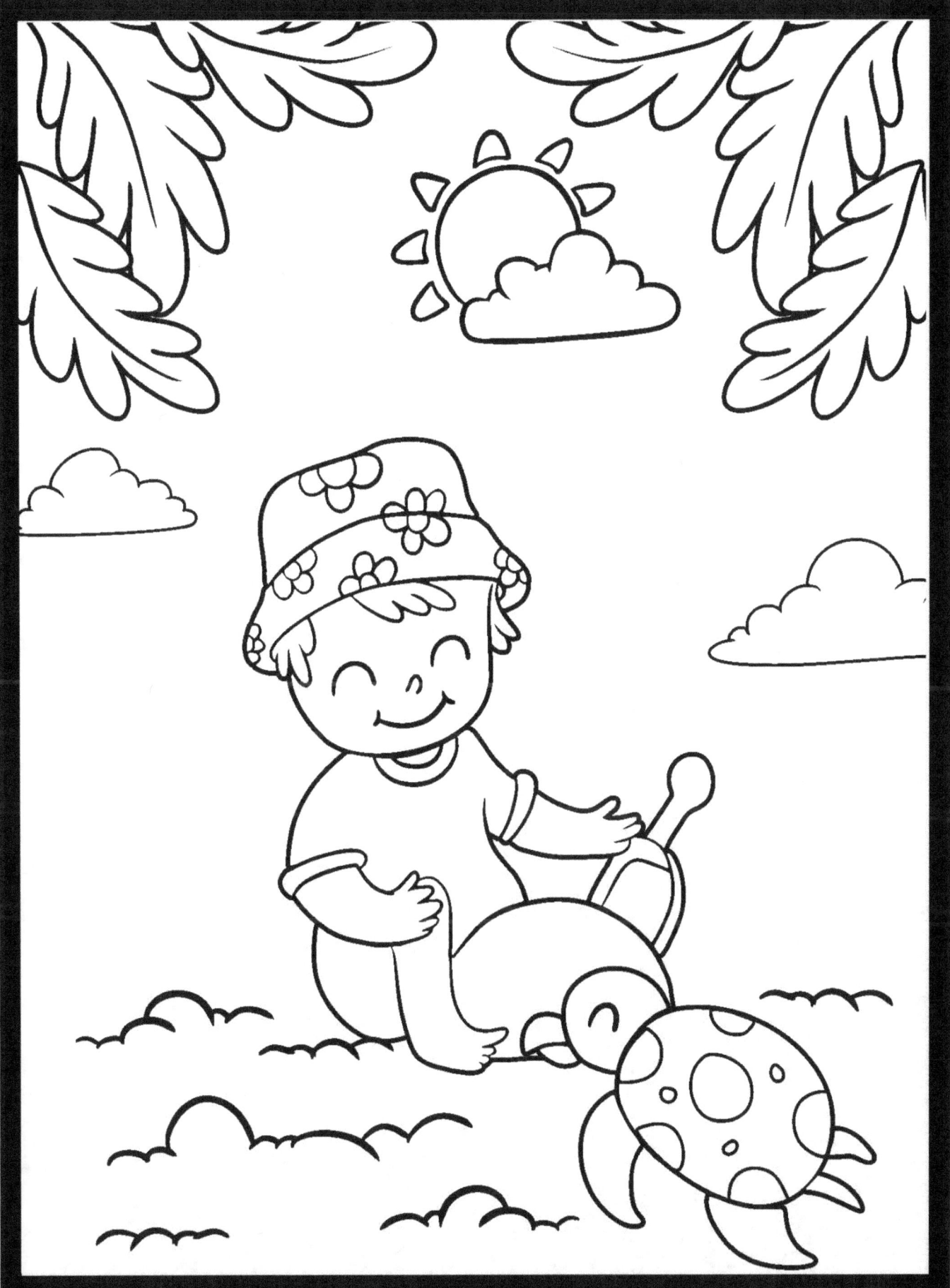

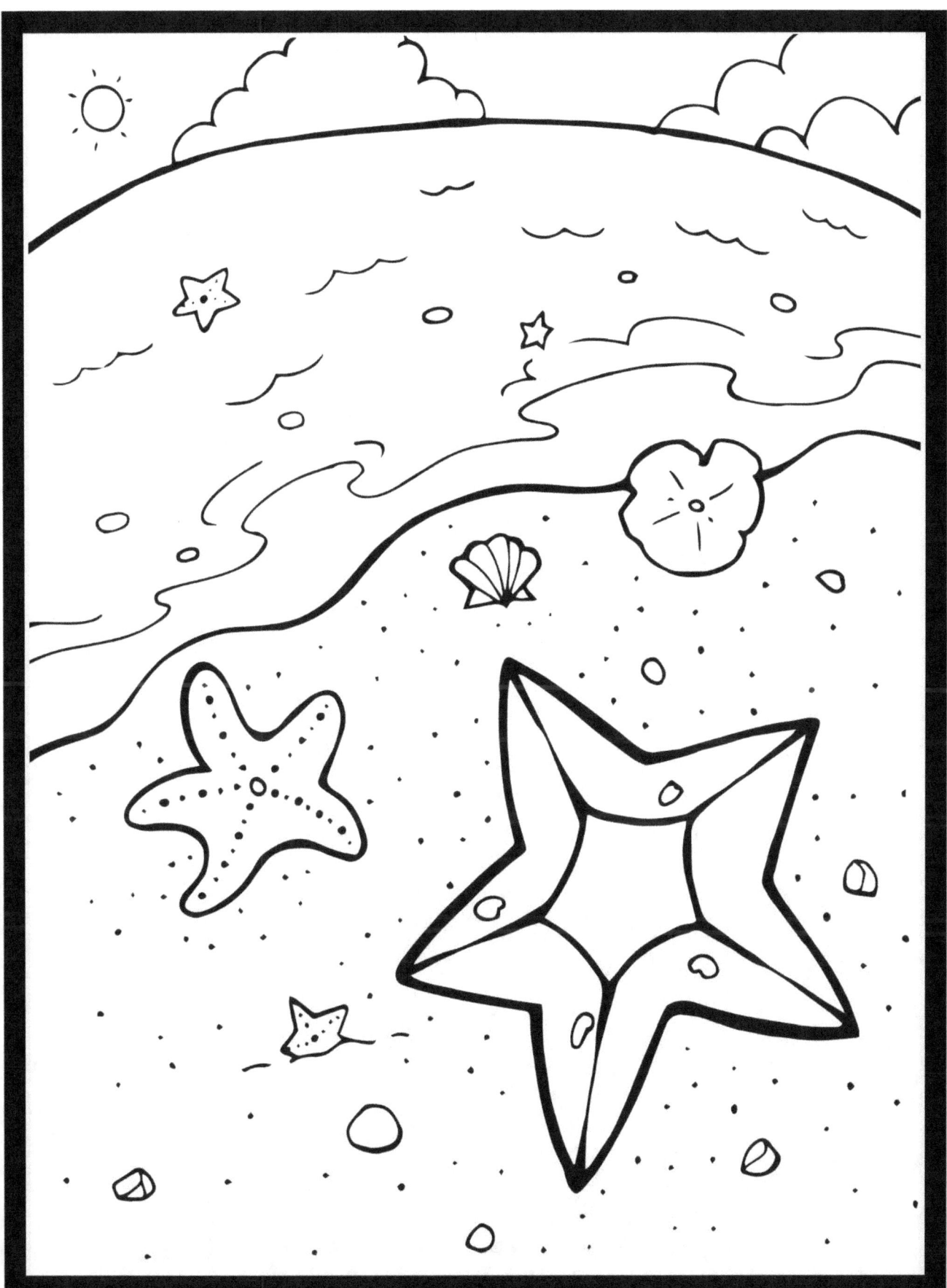

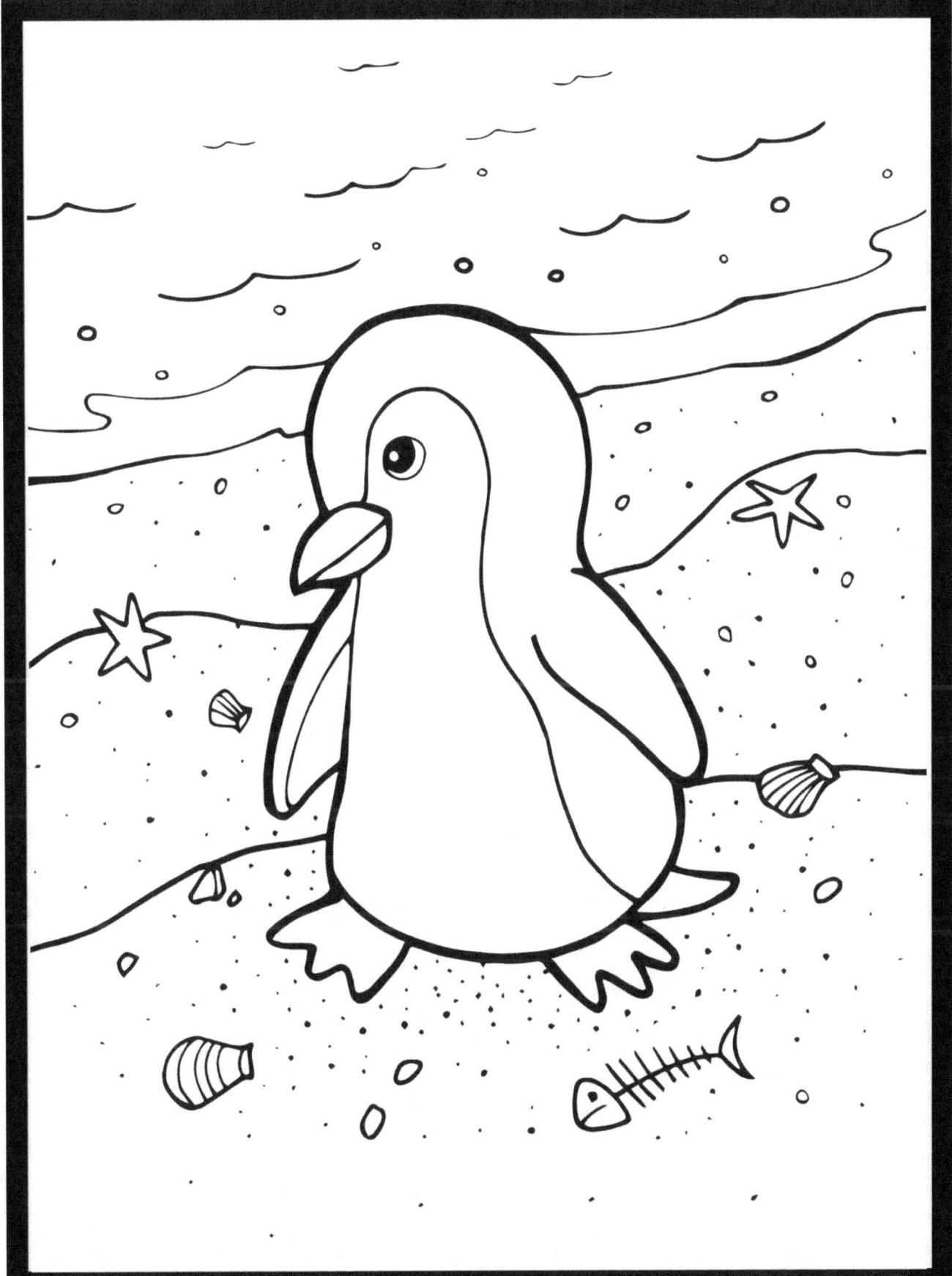

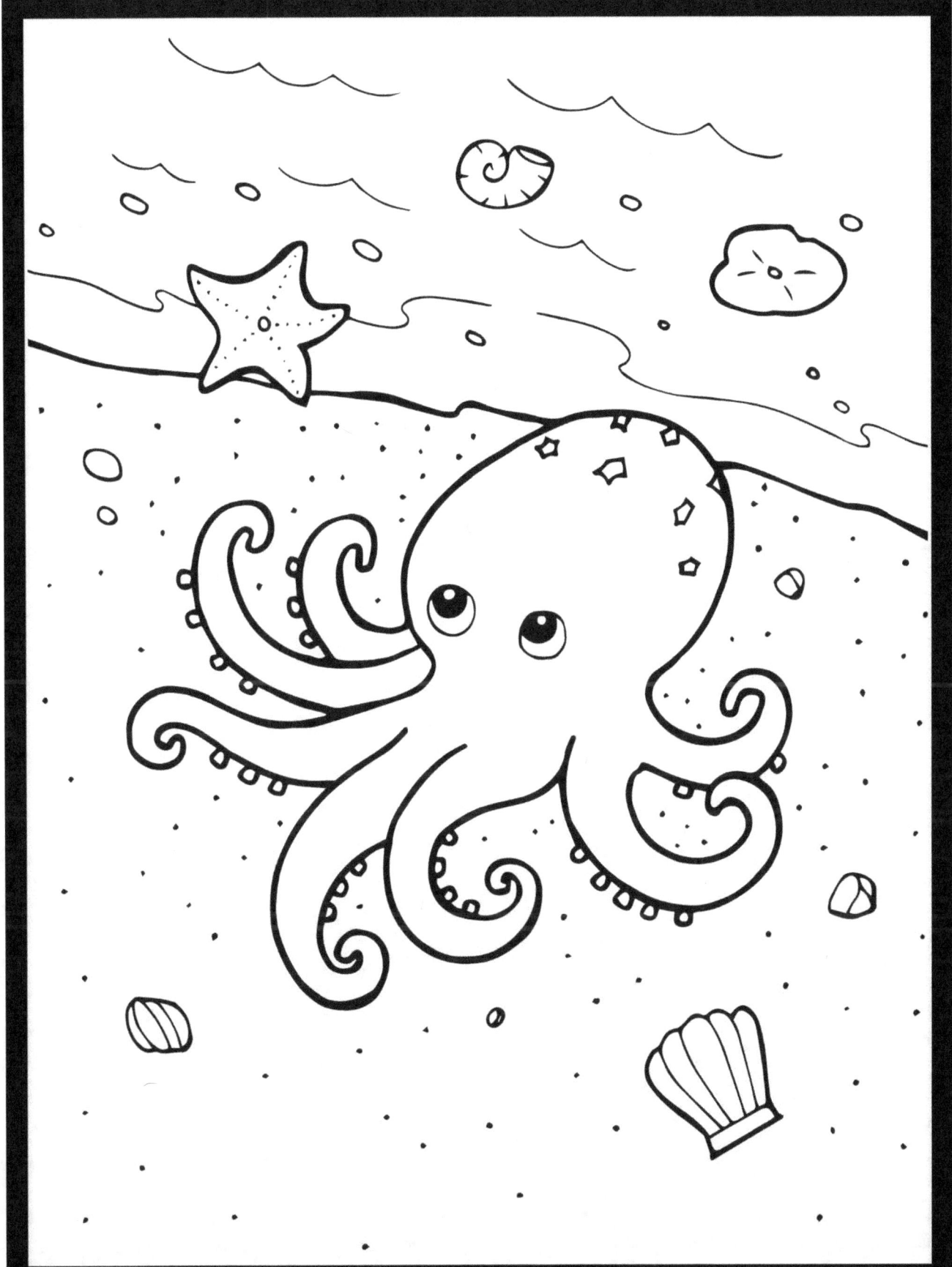

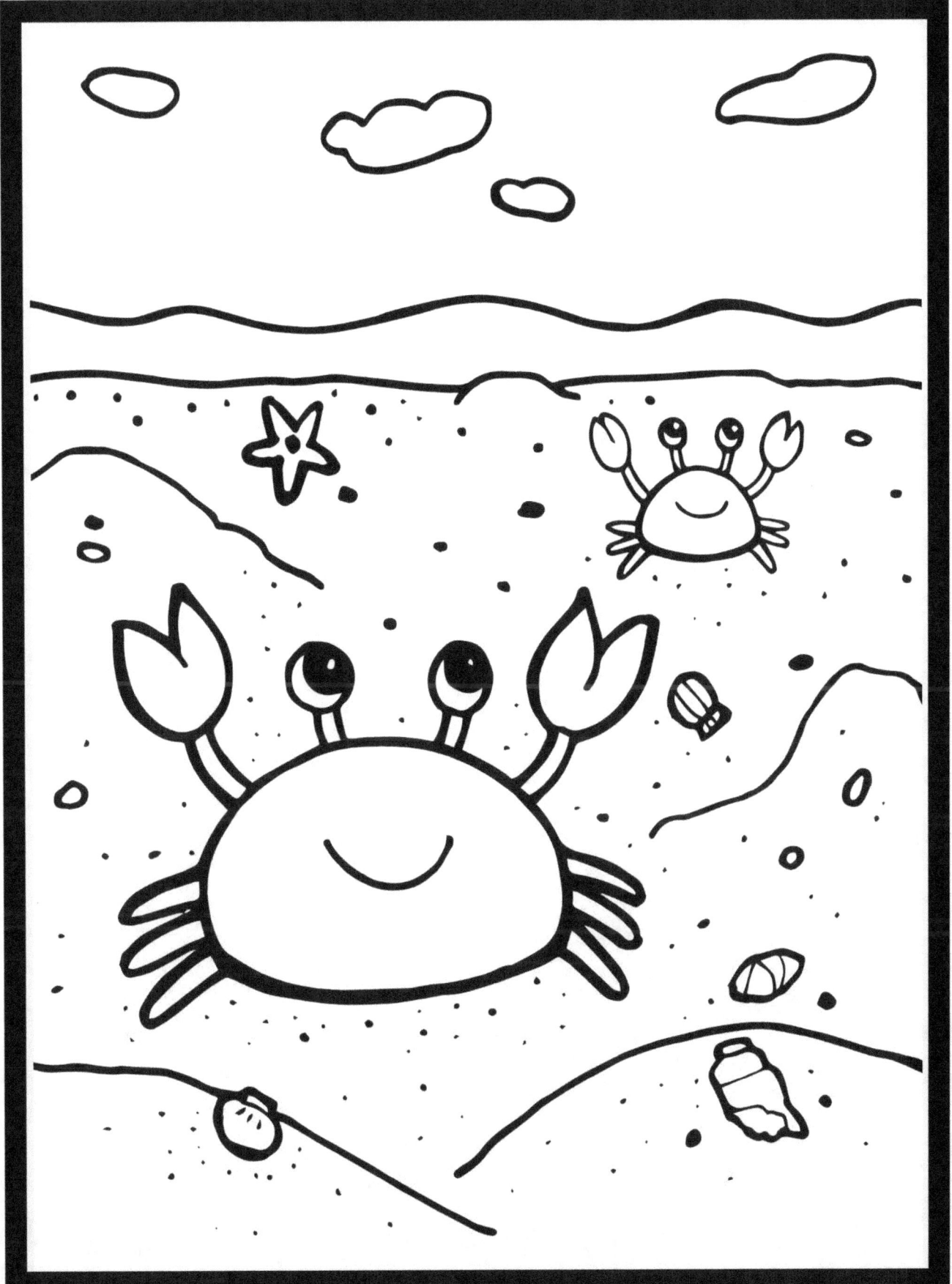

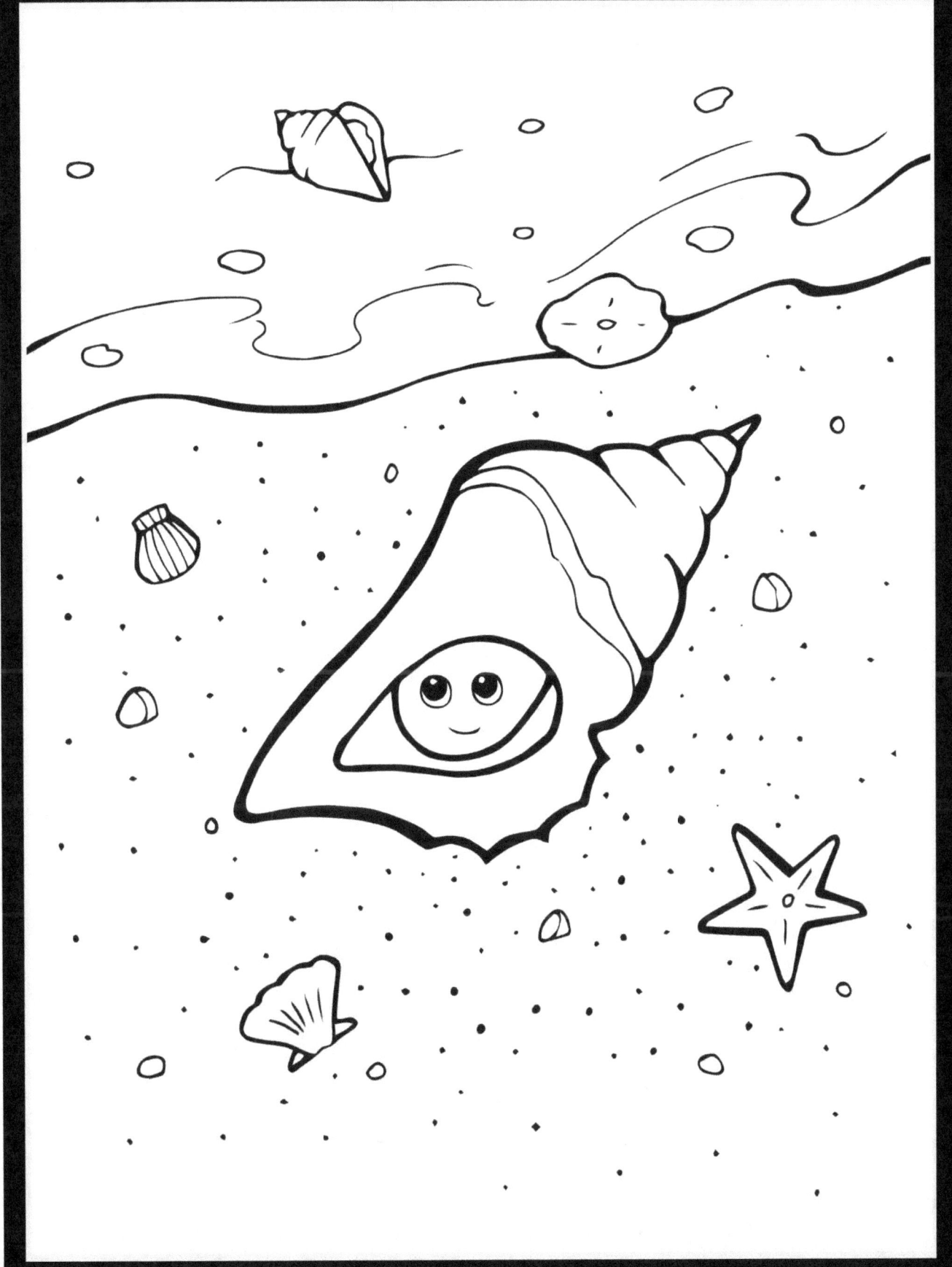

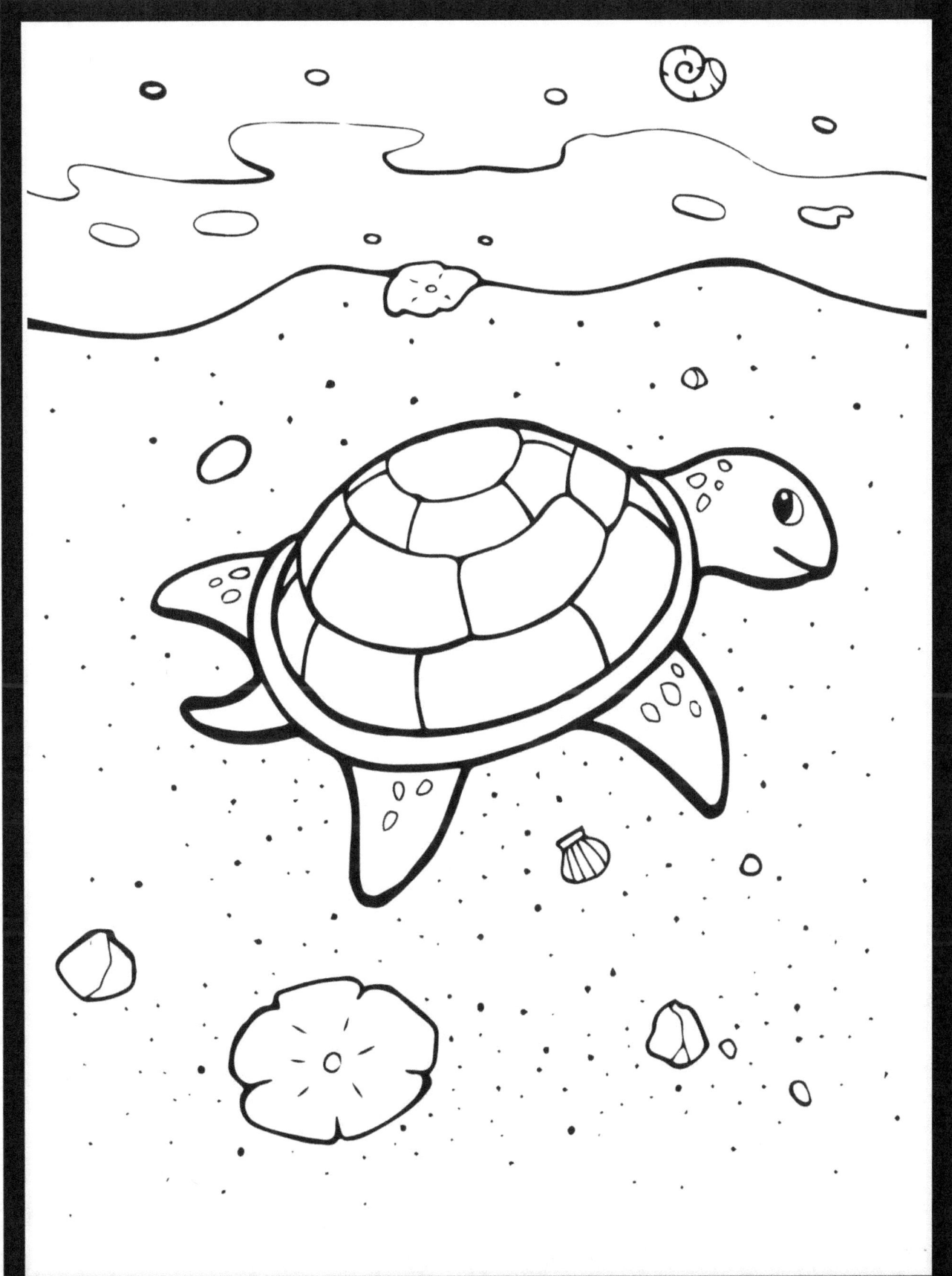

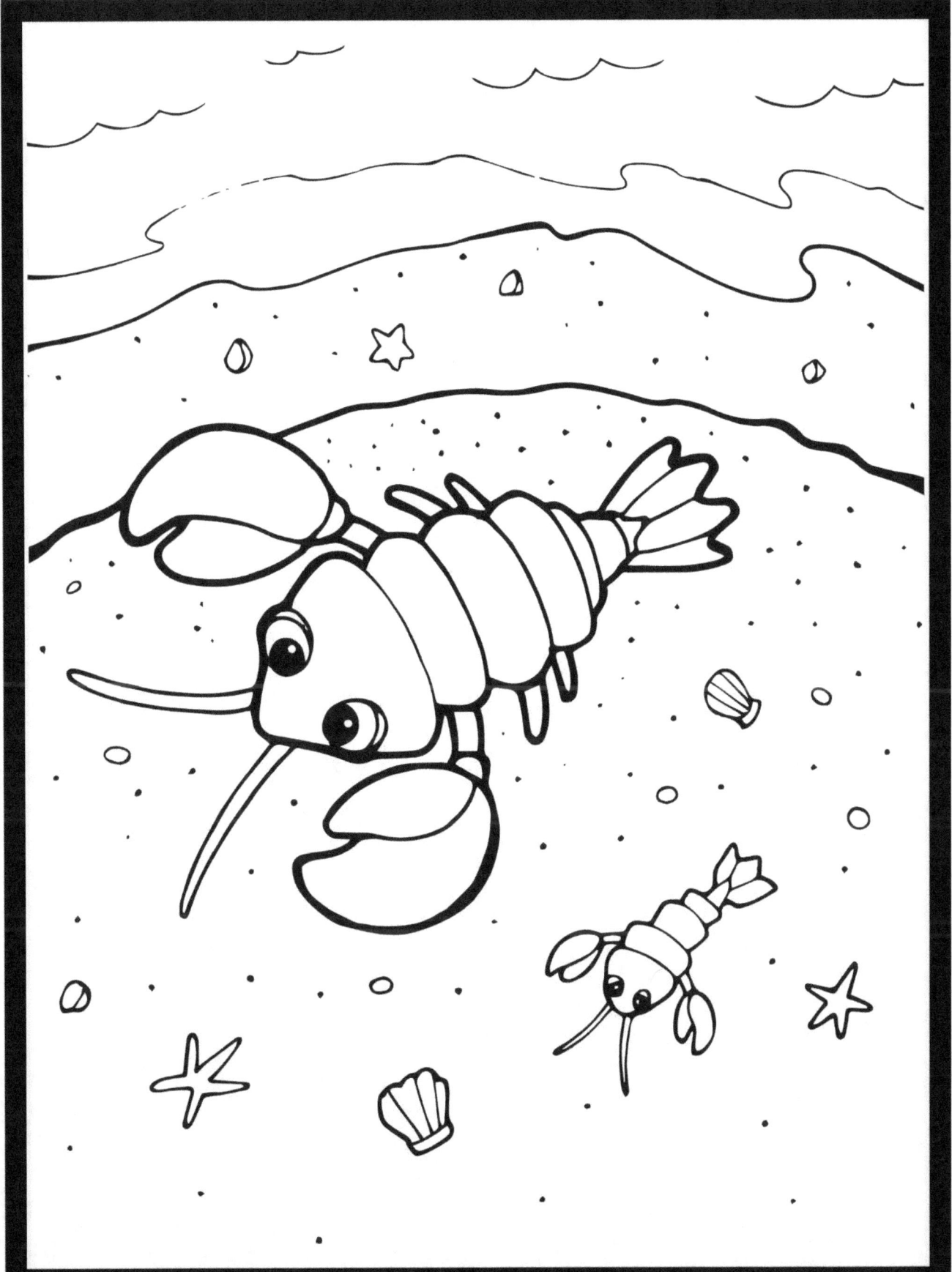

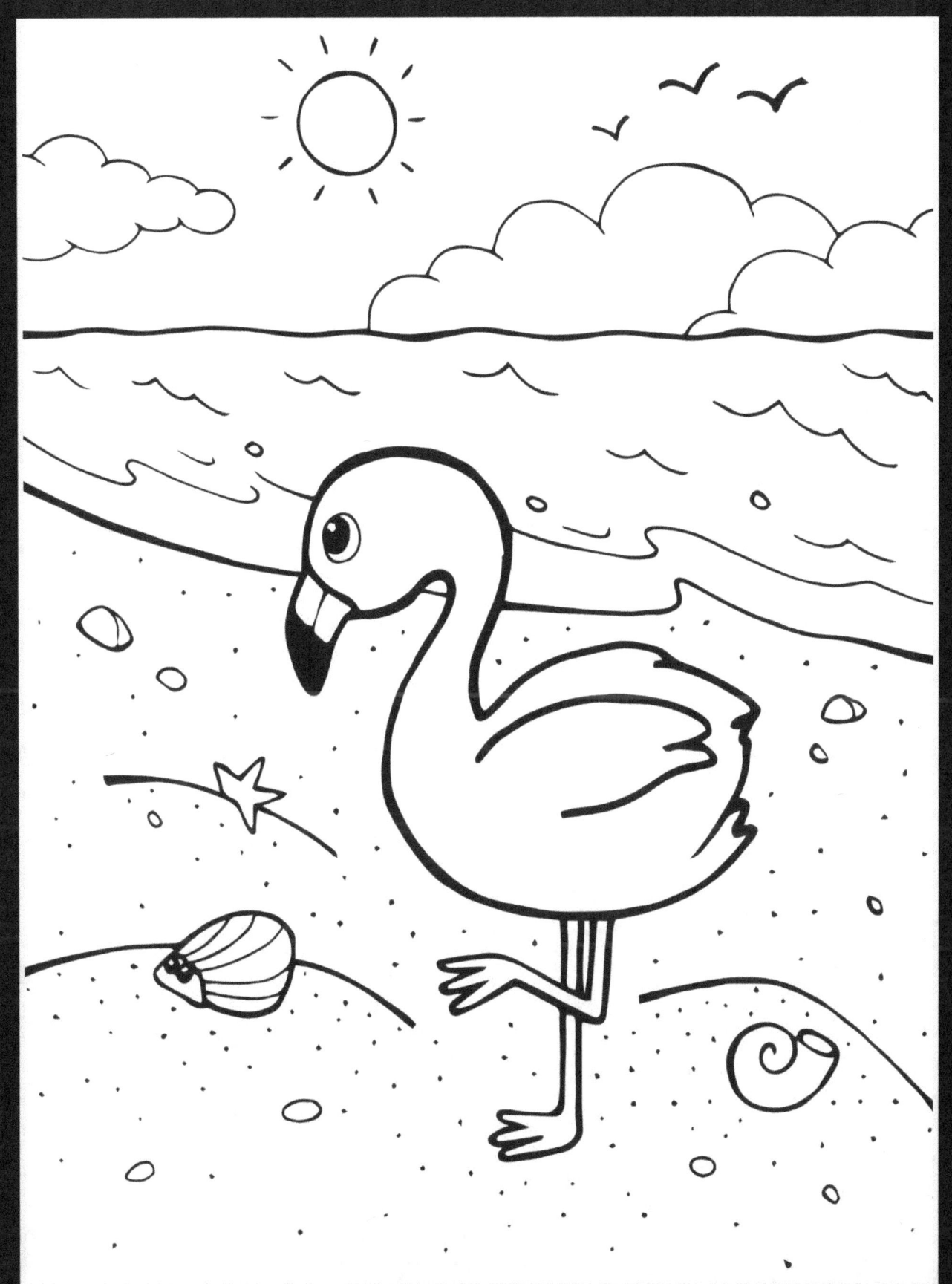

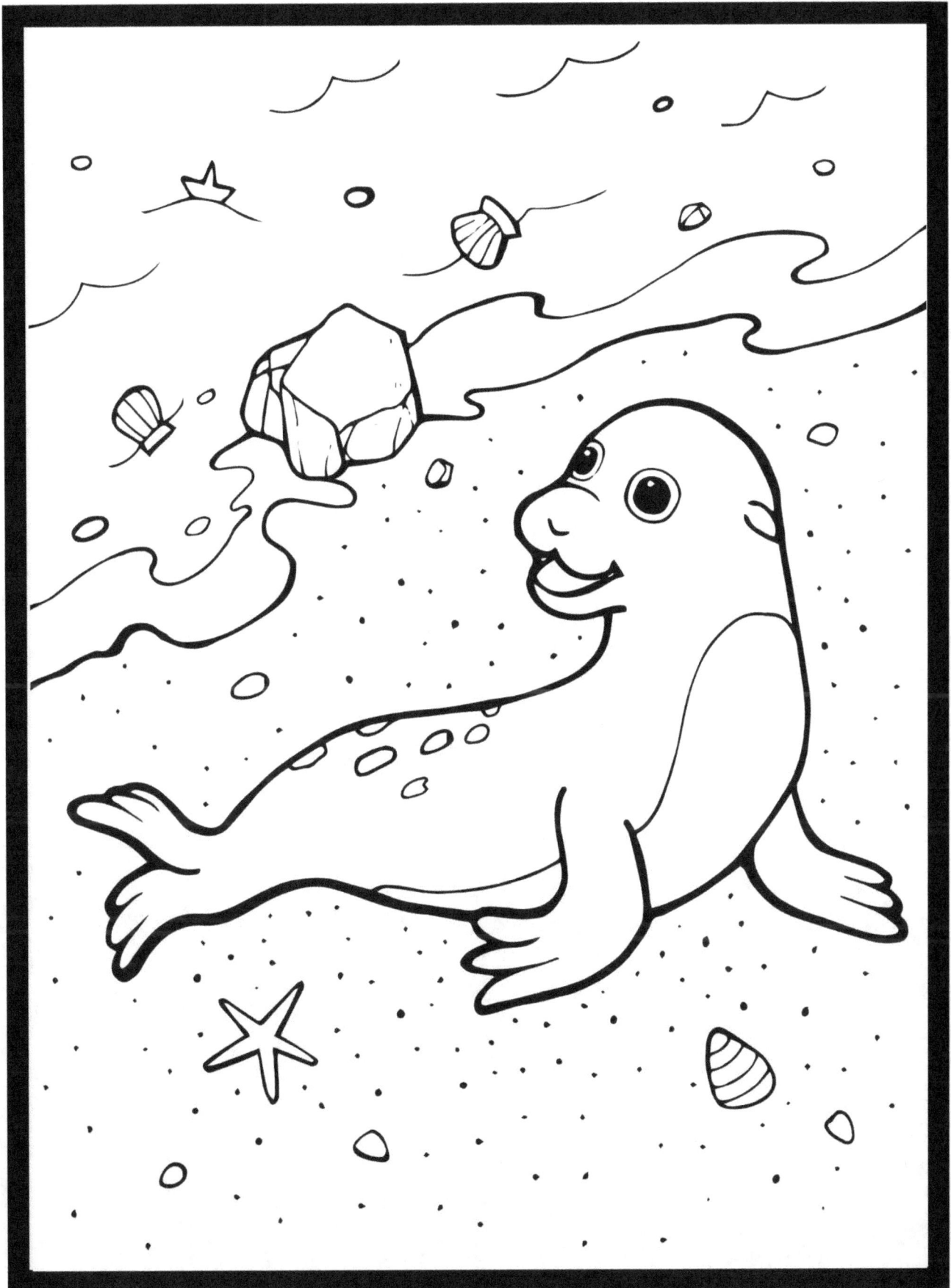

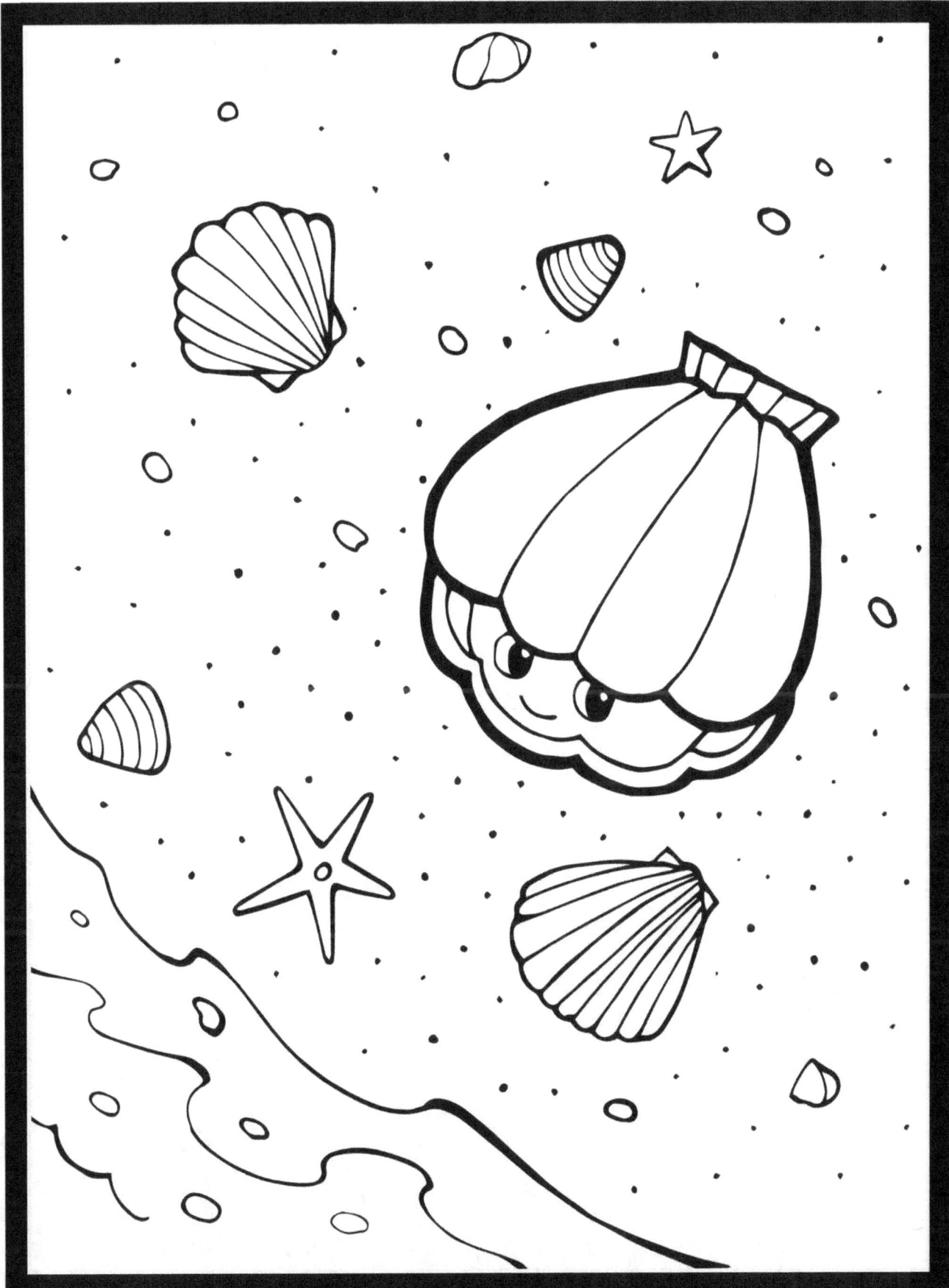

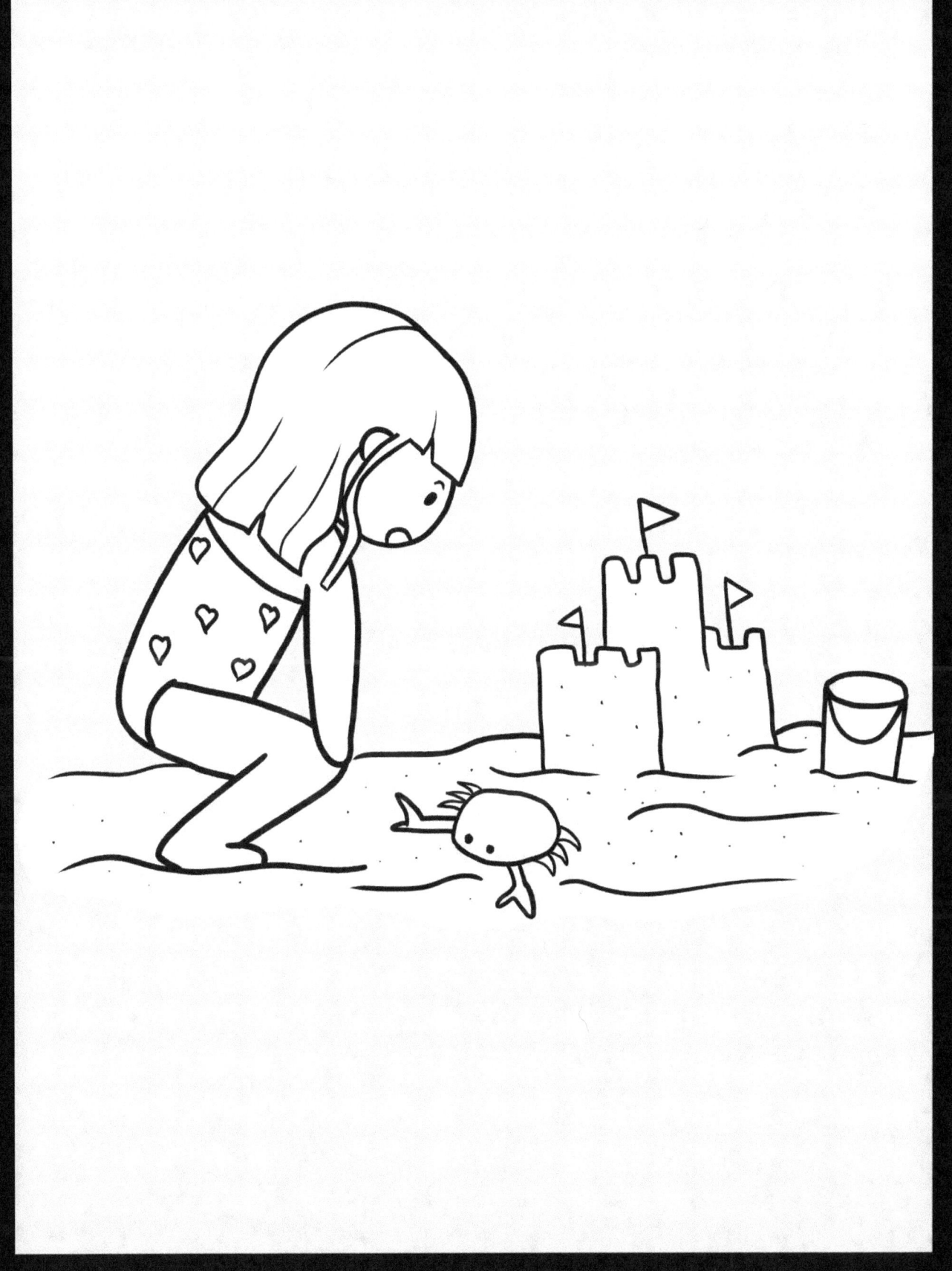

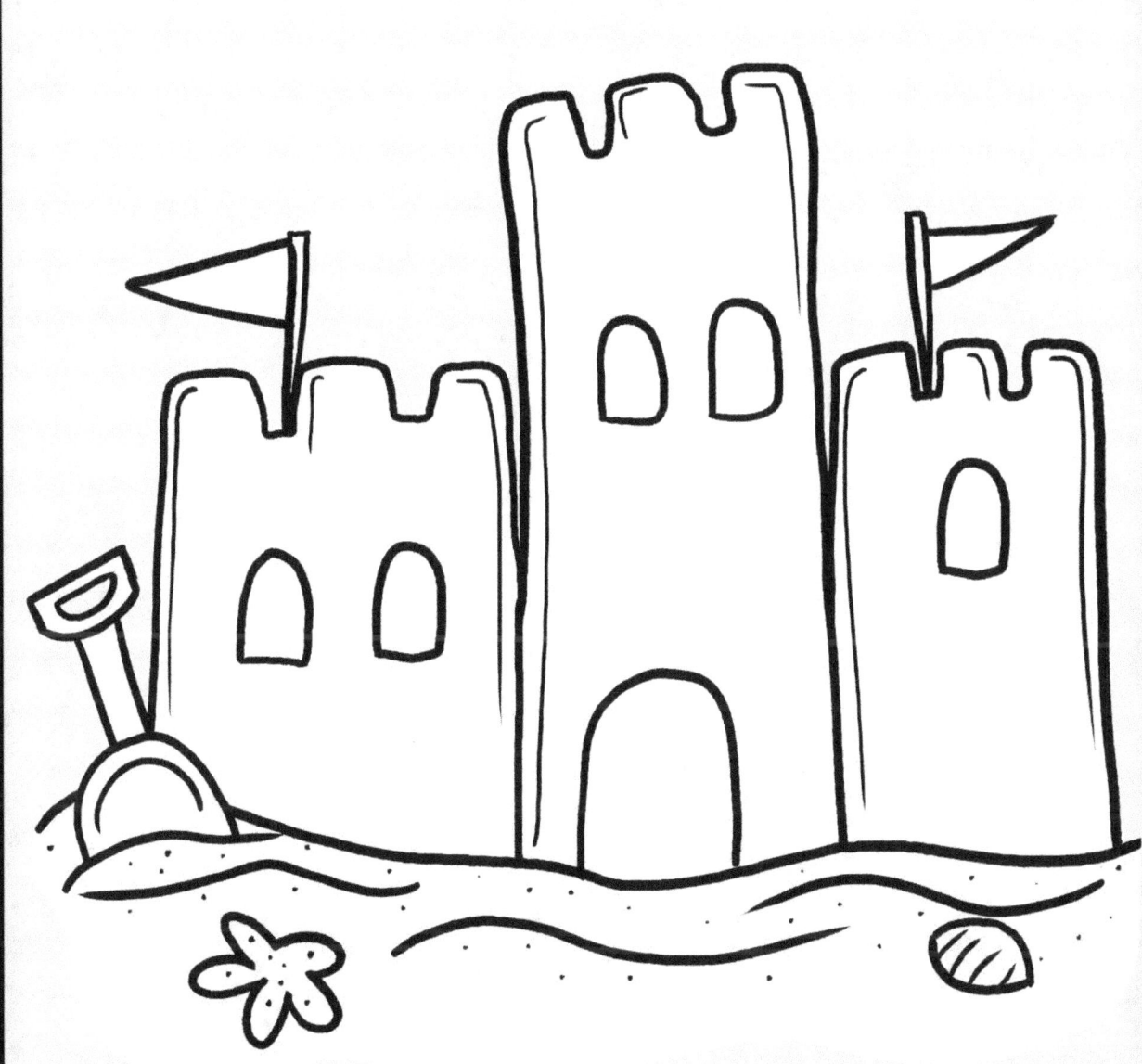

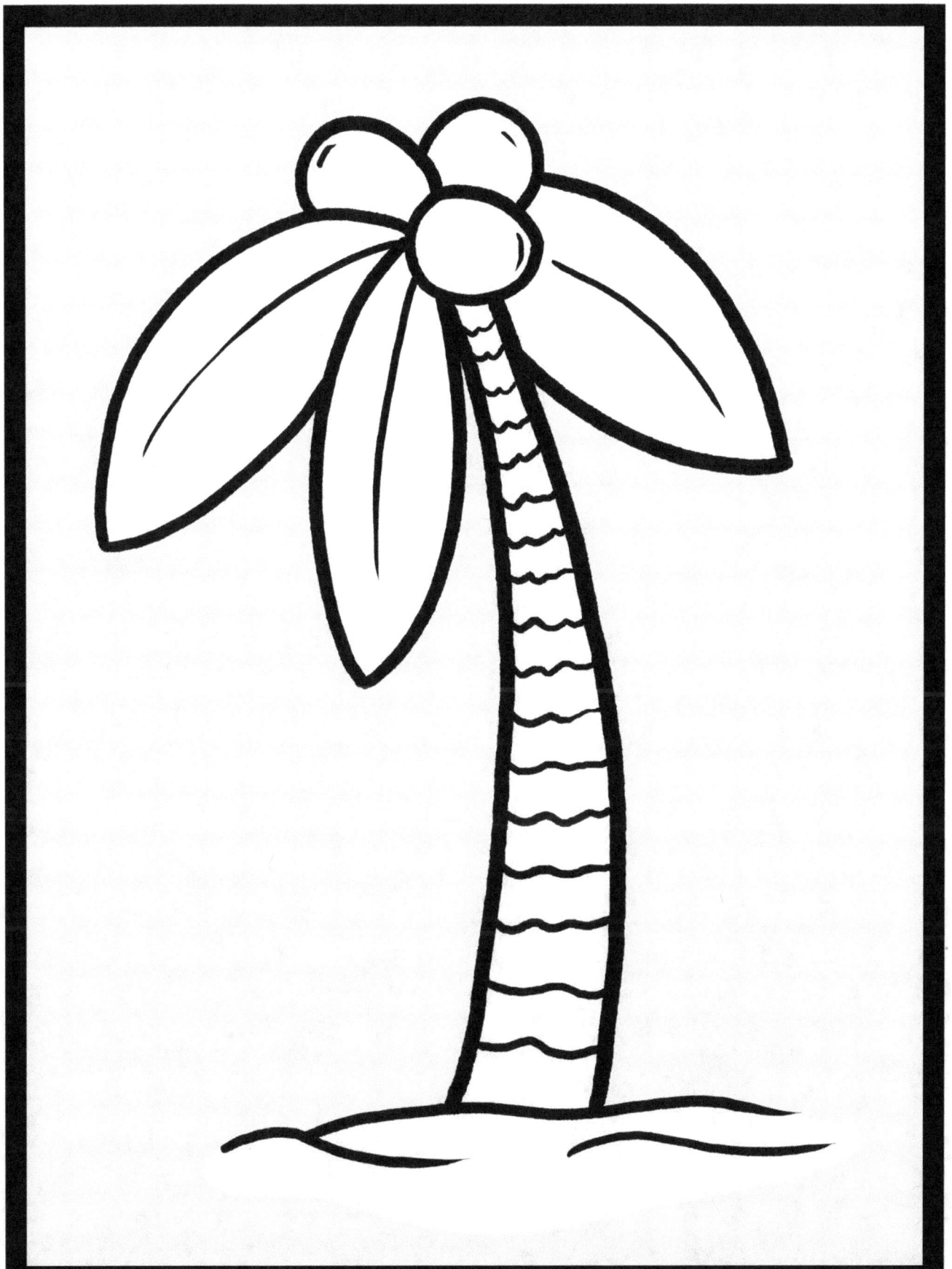

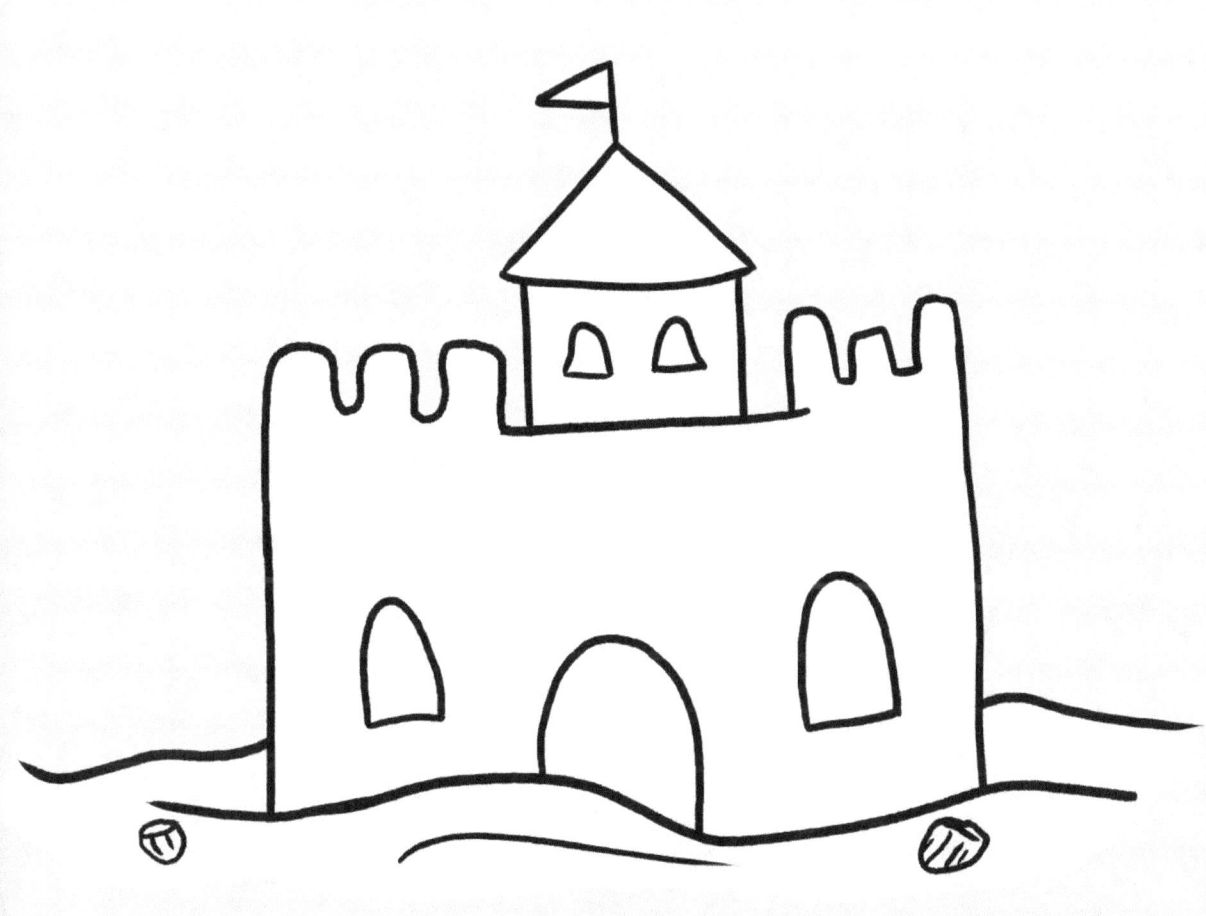

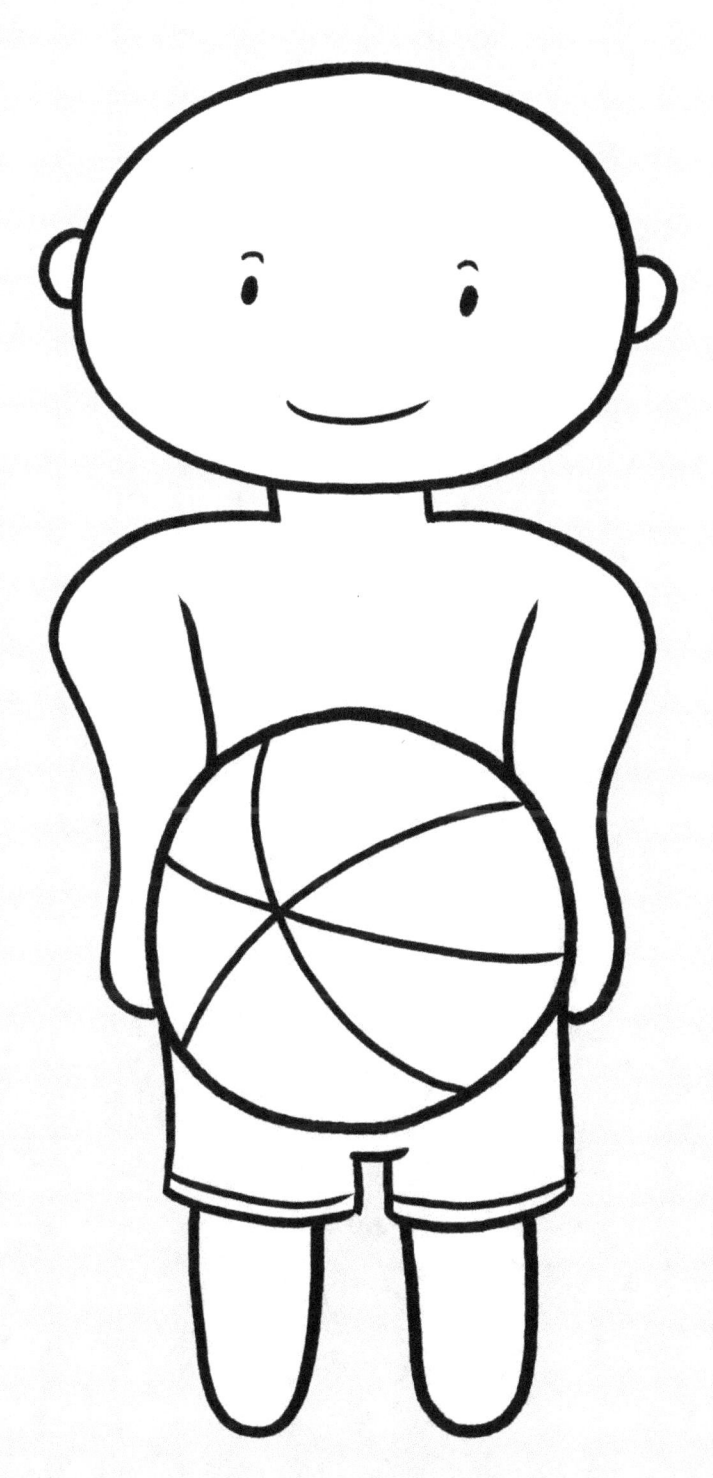

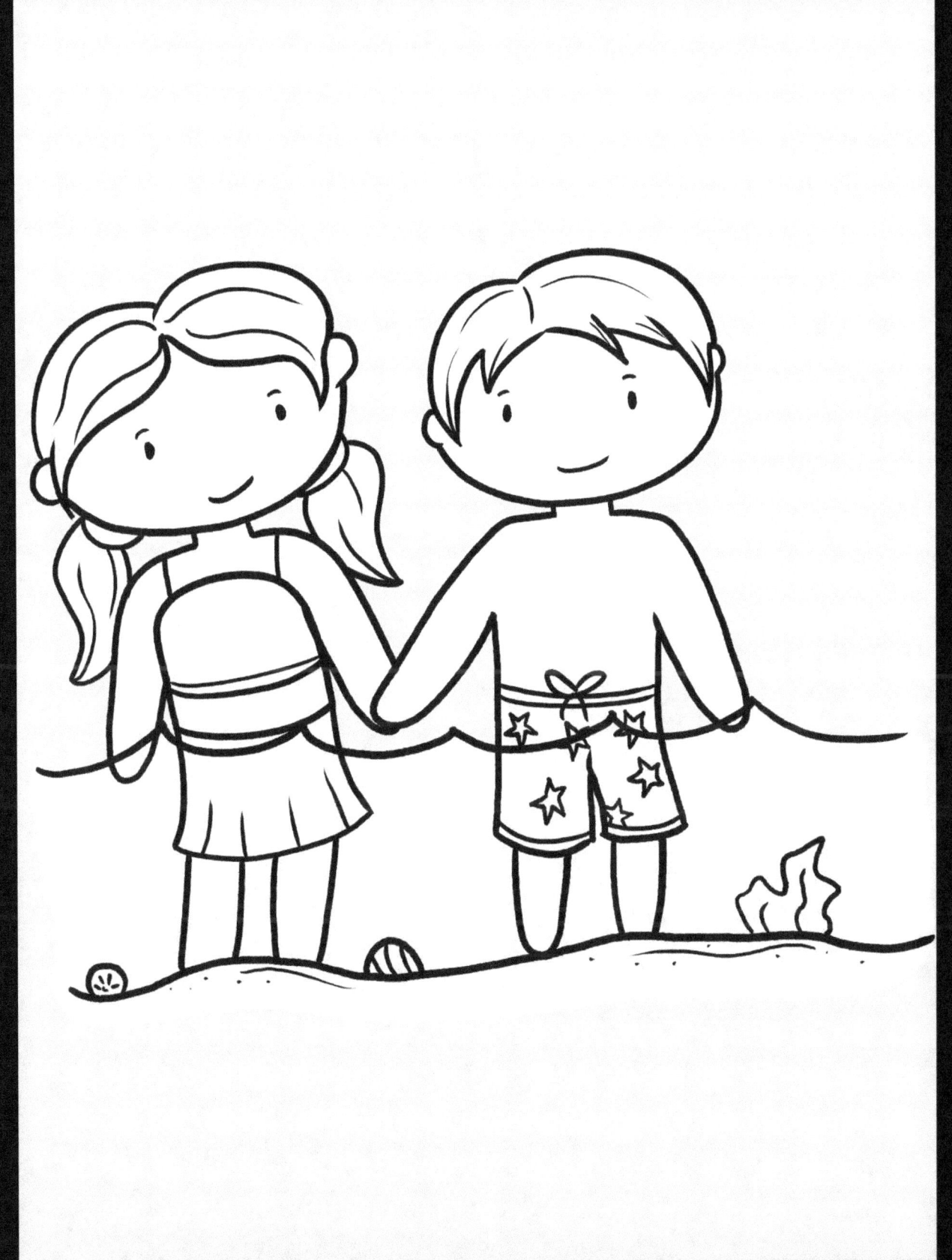

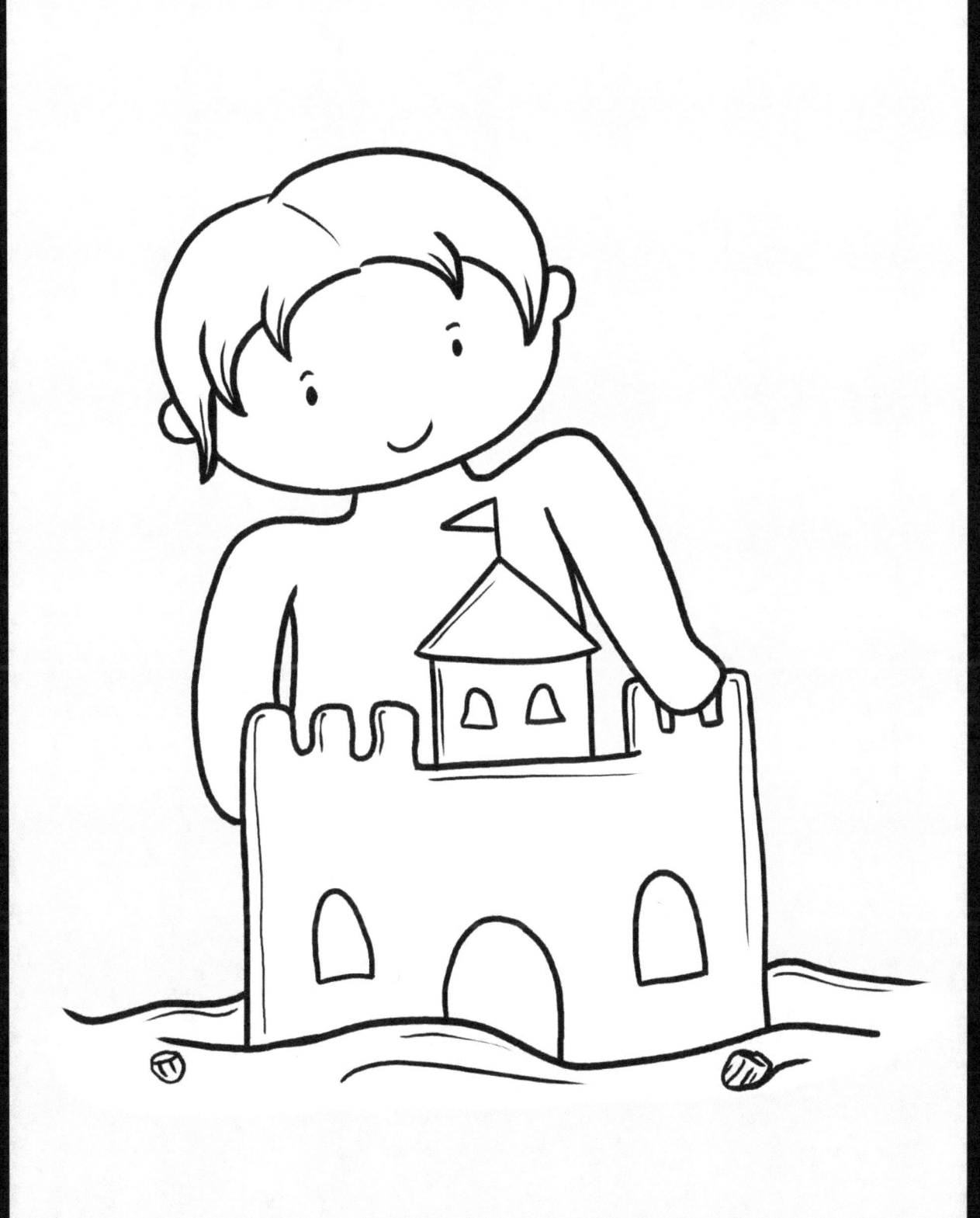

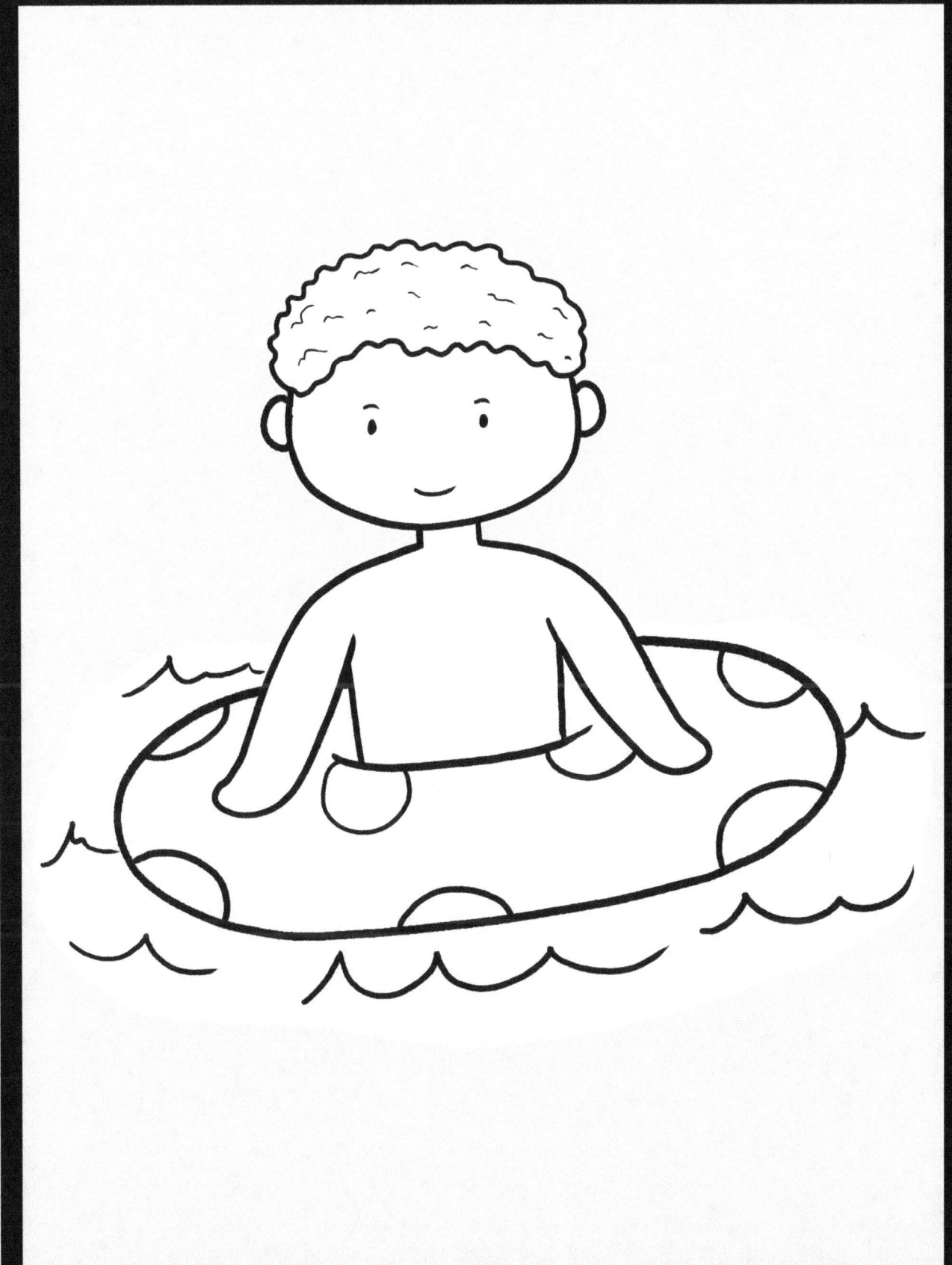

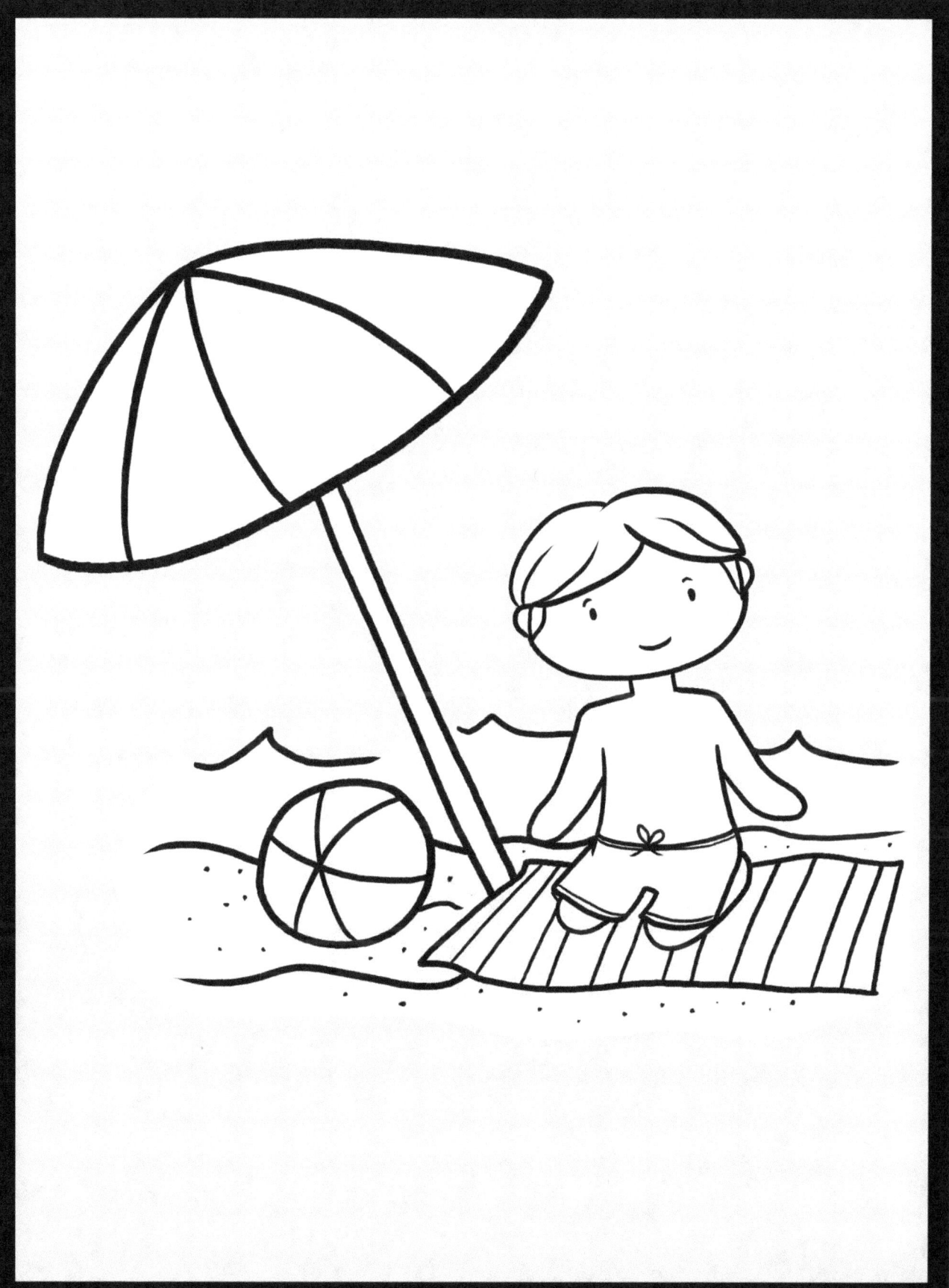

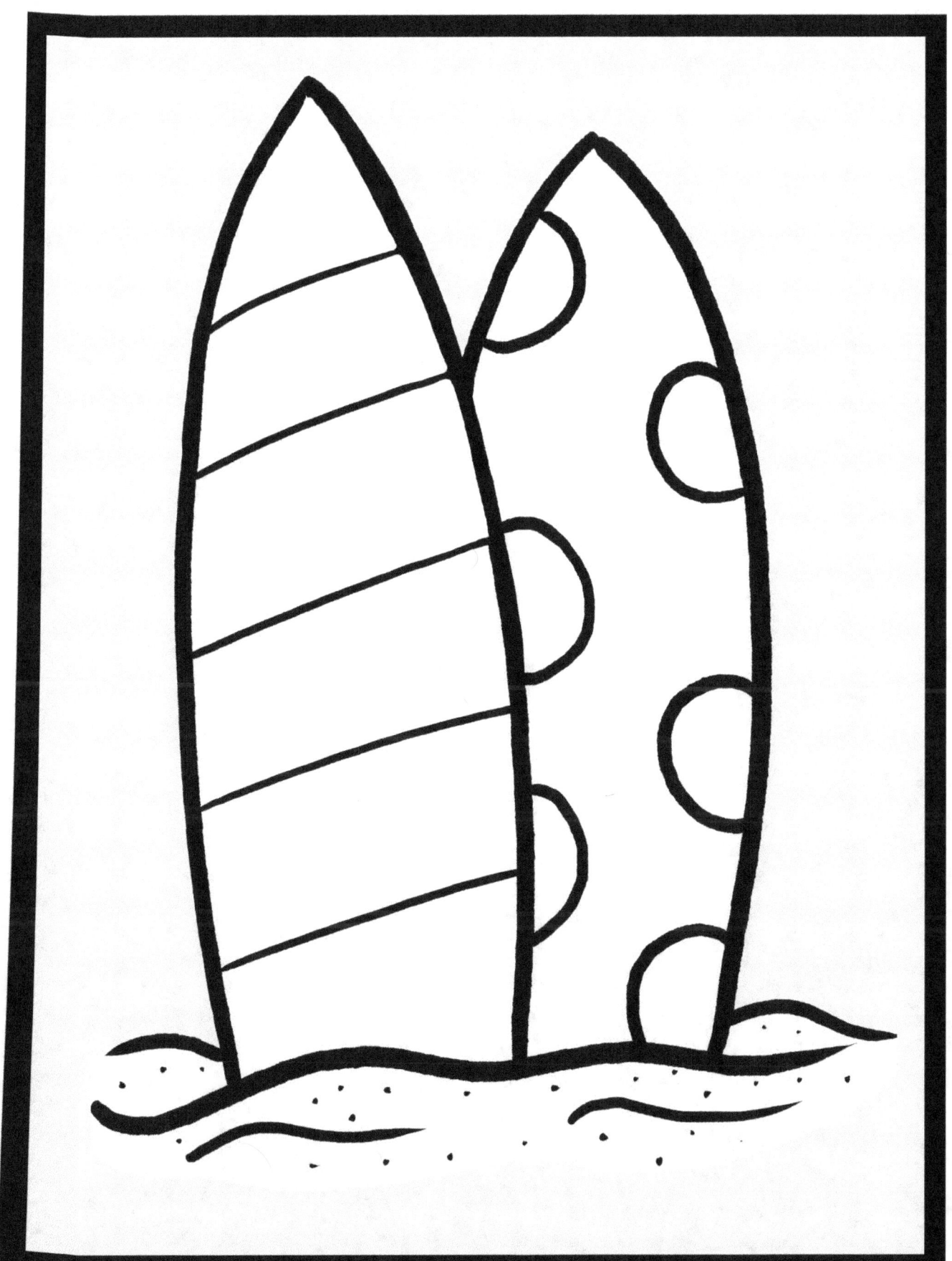